Jesus

The Story
You Thought You Knew

DEACON KEITH STROHM

Our
Sunday
Visitor

www.osv.com
Our Sunday Visitor Publishing Division
Our Sunday Visitor, Inc.
Huntington, Indiana 46750

Our Sunday Visitor Publishing Division, Our Sunday Visitor, Inc., 200 Noll Plaza, Huntington, IN 46750; 1-800-348-2440

ISBN: 978-1-68192-076-4 (Inventory No. T1820)
eISBN: 978-1-68192-078-8
LCCN: 2017930526

Cover design: Lindsey Riesen
Cover art: Renata Sedmakova/Shutterstock.com
Interior design: Dianne Nelson

PRINTED IN THE UNITED STATES OF AMERICA

About the Author

Deacon Keith Strohm is the former director of the Office for the New Evangelization for the Archdiocese of Chicago. A well-known international speaker, he has helped tens of thousands of men and women hear the gospel message and encounter the mercy, love, and power of Jesus Christ. Deacon Keith has extensive experience in creating and sustaining processes and programs of evangelization and formation at the group, parish, and diocesan levels that focus on the making, maturation, and missioning of disciples of Jesus Christ. He is also the executive director of M3 Ministries (www.m3catholic.com) and a longtime teacher and collaborator with the Catherine of Siena Institute. He is a co-author, along with six other collaborators, with Sherry Weddell for the book *Becoming a Parish of Intentional Disciples*—a follow-up to the bestselling book *Forming Intentional Disciples*. You can follow him on Twitter @KeithStrohm.

THE REDEEMER OF MAN, Jesus Christ,
is the center of the universe and of history.

— St. John Paul II, *Redemptor Hominis,*
March 4, 1979

Acknowledgments

Having an extensive background in publishing, I know that every book is a team effort. Despite that knowledge, I'm always surprised at the blood, sweat, and tears that are involved when I am the author. This book emerged out of my experience leading parish missions and evangelization-focused retreats. For inspiration, support (both technical and spiritual), and feedback, without which this book would not have made it past the idea stage, I'd like to thank the following people:

Sherry Weddell, Katherine Coolidge, and Bobby Vidal, for countless hours spent talking, challenging each other, brainstorming, and praying about the need for our people to have a deeper encounter with the kerygma.

Kristin Bird, Father Matt Bozovsky, Rachel Espinoza, Coleen Hamilton, Sarah Kaczmarek, Julianne Stanz, and (again) Bobby Vidal, who read parts of the manuscript and provided commentary, correction, support, and theological insight.

All of the members of the *Forming Intentional Disciples* forum on Facebook for great conversation and the insight that comes with trying to apply principles of evangelization to real life situations and contexts, and all of the pastors and parish communities that have invited me to lead them through an experience of the Great Story of Jesus, whether through a retreat, day of reflection, or parish mission.

Last, but certainly not least, the incredible team at Our Sunday Visitor, who guided this book through every stage and made it so much better than I could have ever imagined—especially Cindy Cavnar, for believing in the idea and helping me get it launched; Greg Willits, for understanding my crazy schedule and not panicking; and my incredible editor, Mary Beth Baker, whose ability to see from the author's perspective and her editorial skill took the blunt prose that I offered and sharpened it immensely.

Table of Contents

How to Use This Book

The Great Story of Jesus is more than a simple tale to be read through once or even multiple times. It is a journey through the deepest facets of reality. This story is meant not just to be read, but to be encountered. When we encounter it with an open heart and mind, it changes and transforms us. The book you hold in your hands is structured to facilitate that encounter. Each chapter takes a section or "Act" of the Great Story and breaks it open. Many of the chapters include suggestions for further reflection, providing a more structured way to "pray through" each of the Acts of the Great Story. There are also questions provided so you can journey through the story of Jesus with a small group.

To get the most out of this book, spend time in reflection and prayer as you complete each chapter before going on to the next one. There may be particular Acts of the Great Story that touch, move, or challenge you more than others. If that happens, take the time to offer that reaction to God in prayer and ask him what he is trying to communicate in that moment. When you finish the story of Jesus, you may want to go back and spend additional time with particular Acts of that story. Listen to that desire.

Like any journey, the more we approach with intentionality and the willingness to be present to what we experience, the more we change. In the Bible, Jesus sent out his disciples on a journey. They went in pairs and announced the presence of God's kingdom to towns and villages. When he sent them, Jesus instructed them to "take nothing for the journey" (Luke 9:3). As you encounter the Great Story in your journey through this book, those same instructions are important. Take nothing for the journey—meaning take no expectations about how the Lord will communicate his love and life to you. If God normally comes to you in quiet and contemplation, don't expect that he will do so in the same way as you go through this book. If God is often present to you in the midst of great activity or in grand experiences, don't assume that this is how he will move in you as you encounter this story. If you've never really had an encounter with the Lord that you can identify, and you often feel that God doesn't speak to you (or that he won't speak), then let go of that expectation. You have begun to read this book. The rest is up to the One who led you here—so be willing to follow where he leads, even (especially!) if it's not exactly where you expected.

This is the Great Story of God's love for you. We know, through the testimony of Scripture and the lived history of the Church, that anyone who encounters Jesus with an open heart receives something. What the Lord desires to pour into your life as you encounter his story may be something entirely new for you. Take nothing for the journey. Leave behind all expectations so that you can receive precisely what he wants to give.

The Great Story is waiting—for you.

Introduction

This is not a book on theology.

Such books, as noble and enlightening as they are, weigh down shelves in libraries all across the world. This is not an extended biblical exegesis or heavily footnoted academic treatise. Nor is this book a spiritual autobiography or written meditation on some aspect of the Christian life. Rather, this book tells a story—a story that can completely alter the course of *your* life and transform it forever.

Stories hold a central place in human culture. In fact, the power of story is prevalent in humanity. From the simple cave paintings of our earliest ancestors, through the oral tradition of storytellers, bards, and keepers of lore, to the great masterpieces of literature and poetry, and even down to the visual storytelling of Hollywood, stories shape our understanding of ourselves and our world. They help to define our identity, give us a sense of a shared experience, and point us to a particular place in the future.

When I was a child, my mother used to spend time reading to me. I treasured those moments as the stories came alive at the sound of her voice. I remember *The 500 Hats of Bartholomew Cubbins* by Dr. Seuss as one of my favorites. Each time my mom finished the tale, I would immediately ask her to read it again. When I grew older and could read on my own, I spent hours each day with my nose in a book. When I finally discovered J. R. R. Tolkien's *The Lord of the Rings* trilogy at the ripe old age of nine, I was hooked. I reread Tolkien's books each year for the next ten years. I lost myself each time in the rhythm of Tolkien's prose, in the epic scope of the story, and in the heroism of the characters who struggled against the forces of darkness and evil. This story had a profound effect on my development as an adolescent, shaping my understanding of heroism, of the necessity of sacrificial love, and of the critical importance of the bonds of affection between friends.

Yet no story contains the sheer power to heal and transform found in the story you will encounter in this book. Why? Because the person at the center of this story is Jesus Christ, the Son of God, who through his life, death, and resurrection broke the chains of sin and death, and who, *at this very moment*, offers each of us meaning and fulfillment in this life and eternal joy in the next.

This is a story of cosmic proportions—of love versus hatred, of ancient prophecies fulfilled, of an apocalyptic showdown between the forces of God and the minions of the Enemy woven into the very fabric of creation. It is the story of the tenacious love of a Father who wills that his children not be abandoned to the consequences of their abuse of freedom. It is the ultimate triumph of meaning over the self-consuming abyss of nothingness. It is, in short, the story of salvation.

This is not an abstract story of a God who is far removed from the struggles and realities of life in the twenty-first century. Instead, "the Word became flesh and made his dwelling among us" (John 1:14), the one whom the prophets called "Emmanuel," literally "God with us." According to Scripture and the unbroken Tradition of the apostles, the Second Person of the Trinity left the glory of heaven to live in the midst of human uncertainty and brokenness, becoming one of us in the Person of Jesus Christ, who is both fully divine and fully human. Jesus experienced the joys and sorrows of this life from the inside, within a human context. He wept, laughed, celebrated, and suffered—dying a bitter and all-too-human death on the cross. This is what the author of the Letter to the Hebrews referred to when he wrote that "we do not have a high priest who is unable to sympathize with our weaknesses" (4:15).

The humanity of Jesus is not an incidental or accidental part of the story. Rather, *it is the entire point of the story!* In his divinity, Jesus reveals the Father to us—a critical act of love. In his humanity, however, Jesus reveals to us what it means to be authentically human. The answers to the questions that we spend our lives wrestling with (or running away from) are found in the Person of Jesus Christ. In fact, this story of salvation confronts each one of us with the reality of our ultimate identity (Who am I?), our ultimate purpose (Why am I here?), and our ultimate destiny (What happens when I die?).

The humanity we share in common with Christ means that we cannot encounter this story of salvation from the outside looking in. Whether we like it or not, we are already players in this drama. When Jesus suffered and died on the cross, he didn't just suffer and die for sin in an abstract sense. He suffered and died for the sins that you and I have personally committed. When Jesus gave himself up to death, it wasn't for an anonymous "humanity," it was a concrete act of love for you and me. And when Jesus rose from the dead, offering the divine life to those who followed him, it wasn't merely to a collective body of believers. It was an invitation to you and me.

This is the good news of salvation, what the early Church called the *euangelion* (literally, "good message"), which in turn was translated into Old English as *gōd-spell* ("gospel" in modern English). Of this gospel, Paul wrote, "It is the power of God for the salvation of everyone who believes" (Romans 1:16), and it is this gospel, this story of salvation, which you will encounter in these pages.

WHY THIS BOOK?

There is a desperate need for men and women within the Church to experience the life-changing power of the Gospel—to know the Person of Jesus Christ, not as a glorified abstraction or an edifying idea, but as the foundational relationship in their lives. We need to live lives radically transformed, released from the power of sin and rooted in the freedom of God's kingdom. Over the past twenty years of speaking and offering workshops and retreats in parishes all across North America, I have encountered thousands of people, many of them cradle Catholics, who hunger for something more in their lives—who long to be healed and set free by an intimate and loving God from the wounds (mental, physical, and spiritual), suffering, and existential fallout that come from living in this world. Some of them would be considered "good" and faithful Catholics, some of them are even daily communicants, yet they struggle with a God who seems distant and a relationship with him that bears little or no fruit.

To be clear, this urgent need for a new emphasis on proclaiming the gospel of Christ (what St. John Paul II called the New Evangelization) didn't arise out of some deficiency in the Church's teaching or sacramental life. Jesus Christ stood at the heart of the apostles' preaching, and it is this very same Jesus who lives at the center of the Church today. In addition, the whole of the Great Story of Salvation is "written" across the Church's sacred art and architecture, in our liturgies and devotional life, and in the writings of the saints.

If we take an honest look at ourselves over the past fifty years or so, however, we have to admit that on a cultural and lived level (what the theologians would call the level of praxis), we have not been so successful at telling all of the Great Story in a way that wins people's hearts and minds. As a result, generations of baptized Catholics have grown up ignorant of the power of the gospel to change them. They are largely illiterate—unable to "read" the whole of the Great Story from within the Christian community.

If you hunger for healing, then this book is for you.

If you long for peace with yourself and in your relationships with others, then this book is for you.

If you are searching for fulfillment, lasting transformation, and freedom from a nagging restlessness that keeps you constantly dissatisfied, but you have no idea how to experience these things, then this book is for you.

Here you will be invited to encounter the gospel of Jesus Christ in a radical new way. Maybe you have heard these biblical stories since your childhood. Maybe they are completely new to you. Whatever your experience, I pray you will meet Jesus in a profound and personal way as you read this book. May the God who fashioned you for love give you the grace to open your heart to the transforming power of this gospel.

CHAPTER 1

The Kingdom: God's Gift to Us

God is love.

Perhaps you first heard that from your parents, or from a religious education teacher. We talk about this reality over and over again in the Church. God is love. We sing songs about it, create banners, read about it in the Bible, and celebrate it at Mass. We surround ourselves with this message.

God is love.

There is a danger, however, in living so closely to something so profound. We can start taking it for granted, growing blind to its beauty and deaf to the radical power of its message. There is an old adage: *Familiarity breeds contempt.* Perhaps those of us in the Church have not grown contemptuous of this message so much as indifferent. We have reduced one of the key truths about God and our place in the universe to a three-word internet meme, and we scroll through our newsfeeds looking for other things to fill up our uncertainty and emptiness, or to make us forget our problems. The truth that God is love no longer captures our attention, or speaks to us of who we are.

God is love.

Perhaps you've never really heard that phrase before. Maybe you didn't grow up in the Church, or you came from a family that never talked about such things. Maybe you've lived your life actively separating yourself from religion and religious groups. Looking at the world today—with global poverty, terrorism, senseless violence, the persecution and attempted genocide of religious and ethnic groups, the prevalence of war and other armed conflicts—it would be very difficult to arrive at the conclusion that there is a God and that this God would be loving, let alone love itself.

But just imagine.

Imagine that there is an all-powerful Someone who loves perfectly—and this Someone created the universe, and you and me, for a reason. What would have to change about how we looked at ourselves? About how we looked at other people? The world around us?

It would change *everything*!

And it is here that our story begins, with the radical truth that we are not accidents or instances of random collections of molecules. There is a plan and a purpose to who we are.

IN THE BEGINNING

Our God who is love wants to communicate with his creation, and he does so in various ways. One of the ways God communicates with us is through the universe and the world we inhabit. Think of a brilliant sunset over the ocean, or the stars in the night sky. Recall a majestic mountain towering over the landscape, snowcapped and rough-shouldered, and the shimmering complexity of a spider's web, dew-dappled and dazzling in the morning light. Our world is filled with beauty, with experiences that take us outside of ourselves and help us to know that there is something beyond our narrowly defined selves.

God also works through the natural processes of the universe to reveal himself. As science and technology deepen and grow their ability to explore, measure, and quantify, scientists are discovering, in the midst of the seeming chaos and complexity that exist at subatomic levels, a precision to the make-up of the universe, particularly at the molecular level. Just a slightly different molecule, or the same molecule in a slightly different position, and the earth would be a lifeless rock hurtling through space. This precision, some scientists say, points to the reality of a designer, a Creator, or an "intelligence" through which the universe came to be. Theologians call the revelation of God through the world and the physical properties of the universe "natural" revelation. Through the use of our natural human faculties, we can come to the reasonable conclusion that there is a Creator. If we only had natural revelation to go on, however, we would miss out on the utterly revolutionary meaning behind our whole existence.

Thankfully, God isn't limited to natural revelation. God's desire to communicate with us is so strong that he breaks into our natural world and provides supernatural revelation, literally revelation that comes from "above" the natural world. One of the ways we receive this revelation is through the Bible, and it is from the pages of Scripture that we launch into the Great Story.

So much of a story depends on its beginning. Beginnings set the tone, conveying a context or background upon which the narrative will unfold. In the opening lines of Genesis, the very beginning of the Old Testament (and of the entire Bible), we hear:

> In the beginning, when God created the heavens and the earth—and the earth was without form or shape, with darkness over the abyss and a mighty wind sweeping over the waters—
>
> Then God said: Let there be light, and there was light. God saw that the light was good. God then separated the light from the darkness. God called the light "day," and the darkness he called "night." Evening came, and morning followed—the first day. (Genesis 1:1–5)

Before anything existed, God *was*. Then God speaks, and where there was nothing, the world as we experience it comes into being. These opening lines of Genesis detail a process whereby God shapes the universe, creating all creatures and placing them upon the earth. The final creation, God's masterpiece, is humanity, represented by Adam and Eve. God declares their creation "very good" and places them in a perfect place, the Garden of Eden (see Genesis 1:31—2:25).

What could possibly motivate a perfect Being, Someone who lacks for nothing, to create other things?

CREATED BY LOVE

It is precisely this question that leads to an understanding of what it truly means for us if this God *is* love. It's true that

God is perfect. Therefore, God's creation of the universe was not motivated by a lack of something within God. It's not like God was bored and listless, therefore he decided to create some things as a way to relieve that boredom. Rather, the opposite is true. God didn't lack anything. He was actually overflowing—overflowing with love, because love is who he is, and love is self-giving. It pours itself out. And so it was out of an abundance of love that God created the universe, humanity, and, specifically, you and me. The very reason for our existence is to experience love—God's love for us, and our love for God and one another.

Why?

Simply because God is love, and love is to be shared and given away. Love always seeks after the beloved.

Pope Benedict XVI reflected on the beginning of the Great Story in an address at the 12th Ordinary General Assembly of the Synod of Bishops in October 2008, and he brought to light a reality that shifts everything:

> All is created from the Word and all is called to serve the Word. This means that all of creation, in the end, is conceived of to create the place of encounter between God and His creature—a place where the history of love between God and His creature can develop.

> The history of salvation is not a small event on a poor planet, in the immensity of the universe. It is not a minimal thing which happens on a lost planet. It is the motive for everything, the motive of cre-

ation. Everything is created so that this story can exist—the encounter between God and his creature.

Think on that for just a moment. You and I are human
beings, not created as pure spirits. The angels are pure spirits.
Neither are we purely material beings. The animals are purely material beings. You and I are different. We are embodied
spirits, a union of soul and body. Therefore, we require a *place*,
a physical creation in which to live and move, otherwise we
would be unable to respond to love.

God knows this—he designed us this way! So, in his act
of creation, he gives us everything—all of creation. From the
densest neutron star to the smallest subatomic particle, everything exists so that we can be in relationship with God and
one another. Perhaps sometimes you are tempted to think
that you don't matter much in the grand scheme of things,
that your life is simply an isolated drop of water in an ocean
made up of trillions of drops of water, and that God has more
important things to deal with than you.

Nothing could be further from the truth.

God created everything with you in mind. Let's put it
a different way: Everything that exists in the universe does
so to serve our relationship with God and with others. That
means you and I (and by extension all of humanity) are the
only part of creation that God made for our own sake. We
don't exist for any other purpose. He made us simply to be
loved and to love him in return.

You matter.

Remember that, in the process of our creation, God
called us out of nothingness into existence. The Lord didn't
just create us to forget us. God didn't wind us up at the mo-

ment of our conception only to set us off and forget about us, like toys that are quickly ignored once the luster of Christmas morning fades. No, in fact, God sustains us in every moment of our lives. The apostle Paul, writing to the Church at Colossae, reminds them of the greatness of the one they follow as Lord: "He is before all things, / and in him all things hold together" (Colossians 1:17).

If God forgot about you—even for a nanosecond—it wouldn't simply be like you suddenly disappeared and your friends would say to each other, "Hey, where did Jeff go?" If God forgot about you, your very existence would cease; it would be as if you never existed at all. Truly, then, God is as close to you as each heartbeat, and God sustains you because of the depth of his love for you.

That's how much you matter to God.

CREATED FOR LOVE

This is the context, the beginning, of the Great Story—that the Creator brought everything into being and created us so that we could be united in a relationship of total and complete love, held in perfect arms and nurtured to become the very best that we were created to be. This is not the story of an absent, distant God. This God is near, and he has thrown in his lot with us. For God spoke into the dynamic, potent swirl that was creation and said, "Let us make human beings in our image, after our likeness" (Genesis 1:26).

Then we read that God "blew into his nostrils the breath of life, and the man became a living being" (Genesis 2:7). The Hebrew word for spirit, *ruah*, means numerous things, including spirit. God gifted humanity with his life-giving Spirit, animating us and offering us a communion of life with the one who made us. For this reason nothing else in creation bears God's image and likeness like you and me. Of all the things that exist in the world, nothing matches the dignity of the human person fashioned in God's image. And if we are made in God's image, then we must understand that we were fashioned to love and to be in relationship.

We know through God's supernatural revelation of himself that God is a Trinity—three persons in one being. God's being is so immense that it cannot be contained in one person. Therefore, God is Father, Son, and Holy Spirit in eternal relationship. The Father loves the Son and offers everything to him—including the depths of his own being. The Son, out of love and fidelity to the Father, offers everything back to him—even his own life. In this mutual self-giving, this Divine Exchange (which has always happened and will always happen), the Holy Spirit is eternally present—the very love between the Father and the Son personified. This is perhaps the deepest mystery of our faith, yet we can speak confidently and say that God is a communion of persons in eternal relationship.

This is why at the heart of who we are is a hunger—a hunger to love and to be loved, to know and to be known. This hunger is a holy one, placed there by God. If you and I are truly made in his image, then it is true to say that we were made to be in relationship, in communion, with God and with one another. It is in our nature because it is God's nature.

FULFILLED THROUGH LOVE

The truth is that our hearts were made for the infinite love of God. God has shaped our deepest desires for eternal things. Nothing here on earth can truly satisfy us at the deepest level. When we don't know this, when even this very first part of the Great Story remains hidden from us, we stumble through life searching in every direction to satisfy this hunger which drives us on. Sometimes we try to fill ourselves up on good things—family, dignified work, serving others. Sometimes we try to fill ourselves up on things that are not so good for us—the pursuit of money, power, sex, alcohol, drugs, or fame. The reality is that whatever we try to do in order to satisfy this hunger, we will always remain fundamentally dissatisfied and "hungry" unless we come to know the One who placed these desires within us.

I recall a time in my life when I was working in the corporate world. I had labored very hard over a number of years to become a vice-president in my company. This desire captured my thoughts and imagination for a long time. It shaped the conversations I had and, in some cases, the relationships I made and maintained. Through hard work and dedication (and, honestly, some luck), I achieved that desire. The very thing that I had worked for over the course of years came through. Naturally, I was ecstatic when this happened. I remember having about three weeks of real satisfaction before I started to feel just the tiniest bit of uneasiness. This uneasiness grew quickly, and it wasn't that long before I was asking myself the questions: Is this it? What's next? Soon, I found myself unsettled and fixating on becoming a senior vice-president.

The point of this little remembrance isn't that striving for things is bad, or somehow ungodly. Rather, the point is I was not satisfied, even after achieving a major milestone in my life. Soon, I was driven to find something else to fill the hunger that emerged. The reality is that only one thing can truly satisfy the human heart: knowing and loving the One who created it. That's why St. Augustine, a disciple of Christ and bishop of the fourth and fifth centuries, famously wrote: "You have made us for yourself, and our hearts are restless, until they can find rest in you."

Think back on your own life, on the times when you've been restless, dissatisfied, hungry for something deeper than the things in your life were able to give you. Perhaps you are experiencing that hunger now. Or perhaps you feel like everything in life is good right now, and there is only an occasional twinge or stab of hunger, when night has settled and the moon has almost completed its course, and the house is silent and heavy with a promise of sleep that never seems to come.

You were made for the One who created you.

That's the beginning of the Great Story. Your life has a purpose, a shape, and a destiny that ends and begins with the love of the Creator who intentionally brought *you* into existence in *this* time and *this* place. He wants so much for you to be in communion with him that he built the possibility of that intimacy within your very being. We hear of God's desire to be in relationship with us in the Old Testament Book of Jeremiah. The Lord is speaking to the young Jeremiah, and God affirms his love for him and his desire for Jeremiah to serve him: "Before I formed you in the womb I knew you" (1:5).

What the Lord says to Jeremiah is true for each and every one of us. We may be tempted to gloss over the stunning revelation that God has offered us. "Big deal," we might say. "So what if God knows us? He's God and knows everything." The problem is that we lack an appreciation for the biblical concept of knowledge. We are not talking about surface knowledge—the knowledge that we might have of an acquaintance or neighbor. In fact, we are not even talking about the knowledge we might have of a close friend. The biblical word translated as "knowledge" from the Greek indicates heart knowledge: in-depth, intimate connection. That's why biblical writers sometimes used it as a euphemism, or "stand-in," for relations between husband and wife—the marital act. As an example, in the Gospel of Luke the angel Gabriel has just appeared to Mary and declared that she will bear a son, and this boy will be the messiah, the long-awaited savior. In some translations of the Bible, she replies, "How can this be, since I do not **know** a man" (1:34, emphasis added).

Here is the depth of God's love for us. He knows us deeply, intimately, and he knew us before we were "formed in the womb"—in other words, before we were even conceived. Before we existed the Lord held us in his heart, knowing everything about us. And while this image is somewhat metaphorical, the radical truth is that the Father waited through the long stretch of eternity for your conception, and for mine. The Father must have danced with joy and delight when we came into being, for at last we could experience the love he held for us. Now at last we could respond and live out that encounter.

From that moment, the Father's arms have been open wide. He knows your name and who you are, and he has been calling you to a relationship that will ignite the deepest parts of who you are and fill you with peace, fulfillment, joy, wholeness, and a perfect love beyond all imagining. The power of this story lies, in part, in its immediacy. This life-changing relationship is not just a promise for a time when our earthly life is over. No, the Lord wants us to experience this peace, joy, fulfillment, wholeness, and healing now, in this life.

The Bible is filled with the proclamation of the possibility of this relationship. The books of the Bible, especially the New Testament, have a language and a description for the experience of this relationship. In Scripture, it is called the kingdom of God. You and I were created for this kingdom. It has been prepared for you and is waiting for you—this kingdom which begins on earth and lasts for all eternity.

It is your birthright.

Are you willing to follow the arc of the story and claim it?

FURTHER REFLECTION

Take some time (at least fifteen minutes a day) to reflect on any of the following Scriptures over the course of the next few days and weeks. If you have never really opened the Bible and spent time prayerfully reading, don't stress about it. Simply copy and paste these references into your search engine, print them out, and read them.

- Jeremiah 29:11–15

- Matthew 11:28–30

- Luke 12:22–34

- Psalm 139

- John 15:9–17

- Romans 8:31–39

You might find it helpful to pray for a few minutes before reading these Scriptures and ask the Lord specifically for the grace to receive exactly the message he is trying to communicate to you at this time in your life. Then, read the specific passage slowly and prayerfully several times. Take note of any words or phrases that jump out at you.

When you are finished reading the passage, ask the Lord to shed more light on the word(s) or passage that jumped out at you. Ask God to reveal to you what, specifically, that word or phrase might have to do with your life right now.

SMALL GROUP QUESTIONS

1. If God truly is love, then the various ways that we experience authentic love are encounters with God. What are some of the ways that you have experienced love in your life? Which ones have had the most profound effect on you?

2. How would you characterize your relationship with God (in other words, if a friend asked you to describe what it's like to be in a relationship with God, how would you respond?)

3. How would you describe the love that a parent has for a child? Do you find it difficult to believe that this is the kind of love that God has for you? Why or why not?

4. Consider the truth that God, as Trinity, is eternal relationship, and that since you were made in God's image, you were created with a hunger to love and to be loved. What are some of the ways that you have sought to fill that hunger in your life?

5. Is it difficult for you to receive the love that God has for you? Why or why not? What are some of the obstacles that you have in your life to receiving that love? What are some things in your life that make it easier for you to receive that love?

6. Name one thing that you hope to get out of reading this book and reflecting on it in a small group.

7. If you have had the opportunity to reflect on the Scripture passages in the Further Reflection section, which passages did you prayerfully read, and what struck you or moved you when you read those passages?

CHAPTER 2

Jesus:
The Embodiment of the Kingdom

S tories require conflict, otherwise they wouldn't be stories at all.

Something—a problem, person, or situation—must provoke the hero, present an obstacle, or oppose the hero in some way. Conflict fuels the narrative of every classic story, and nowhere is that more true than in the Great Story.

Conflict enters the scene early on. In fact, the beginning of our story has hardly finished before things get out of hand. God fashions the universe and populates the earth, and he places the crowning jewel of creation, his masterpiece, Adam and Eve, in a paradise where Creator and creature enjoy an intimate connection. We read in the Book of Genesis that God put man in the garden to "cultivate and care for it" (2:15) not simply as a hired hand or professional worker but as a partner.

We see the level of trust God places in man in this key passage: "So the LORD God formed out of the ground all the wild animals and all the birds of the air, and he brought them to the man to see what he would call them; whatever the man called each living creature was then its name" (Genesis 2:19). In the biblical worldview, to name something was to have power over it, to give it shape and identity. By tasking Adam with naming the animals, God treats man as a partner, making him a steward and inviting him into a communion of life. In the beginning, there is deep connection and integrity, harmony and communion between God and man, and between man and the created world.

That communion extends to the relationship between man and woman as well. At the beginning of our story, Adam and Eve possess a deep communion with each other, a wholeness and mutuality characterized by intimate self-gift. We see this intimacy represented in the second account of the creation of man and woman in the Book of Genesis. After fashioning Adam from the clay of the earth, God knows that it is "not good for the man to be alone" (2:18), and creates a companion, a helpmate, a partner. Placing Adam in a deep sleep, the Lord God forms Eve out of one of Adam's ribs. That is why Adam exclaims with such awe, "This one, at last, is bone of my bone / and flesh of my flesh" (2:23). In Eve, Adam sees one who is his equal in dignity, another person who is both different from himself and yet alike in the deepest of ways. For Adam, Eve is not simply other; she is beloved. The author of Genesis affirms this experience of integral intimacy and connection between Adam and Eve: for the "man and his wife were both naked, yet they felt no shame" (2:25).

Adam and Eve enjoy interlocking "webs" of communion in the Garden of Eden—communion with God, with creation, and with each other. In the garden, the love relationship between God and his creatures is to be lived out for all eternity. Adam and Eve have complete access to every wonder of the garden. God gives everything to them, with just one exception: they must not eat of the fruit of the Tree of the Knowledge of Good and Evil.

As we journey into the second chapter of our story, this may seem like an arbitrary rule God simply drops on Adam and Eve. However, consider for a moment what this forbidden fruit symbolizes. God, by definition, is an eternal being—without a beginning or an end. Humanity, however, has a clear beginning. Therefore, we are not gods, and even though twenty-first-century culture focuses a great deal on self-determinism and choosing one's identity, we are not the beginning and the end of our destiny, nor are we in complete control over what we experience. We are creatures, fashioned and made by a God who loves us, yet still creatures. The Tree of the Knowledge of Good and Evil, therefore, represents the limits of our creaturehood—our finitude.

It is precisely here that the drama of our story begins.

Satan—once the brightest angel named Lucifer who, upon learning of the divine plan for humanity and all creation, refused to submit to God's will—invades the Garden of Eden, coming as a serpent to whisper lies into Eve's ears. The Enemy immediately strikes at the heart of her relationship with God. He asks her if she and Adam are forbidden to eat the fruit of every tree in the garden. Already, we see the trust Eve has in her Creator begin to dissolve. She replies that they may eat of all the trees except one, and if they eat the fruit of that tree, or even touch it, they will die. However, God's prohibition only mentions eating of the tree. Eve's response is untrue. Even the serpent's initial question about God's commands starts to affect Eve. Her response does not reflect the loving trust of a daughter, but rather the attitude of one whose relationship with God is tinged with fear.

The devil launches his next attack: "But the snake said to the woman: 'You certainly will not die! God knows well that when you eat of it your eyes will be opened and you will be like gods, who know good and evil'" (Genesis 3:4-5). This is often the devil's preferred tactic, insinuating that God isn't a good Father, but rather a jealous and imperfect one. When Satan utters those words, the trust Eve held for God continues to die in her heart. Looking at the tree, she sees that its fruit is delicious and good to eat. *Surely, **if** my Father were a good Father, he would want me to enjoy the best food.*

Eve also sees that the fruit is beautiful to behold. *Surely, **if** my Father were a good Father, he would not want to deny me beauty.*

Finally, Eve sees that the fruit is good for gaining wisdom, the knowledge of good and evil. *Surely, wisdom is a precious thing to have, and **if** my Father were a truly good Father, he would not withhold wisdom from me.*

Turning her back on God, Eve takes the fruit, gives some to Adam, and they both eat it, deliberately choosing to disobey God. Remember, the Tree of the Knowledge of Good and Evil represents the limits of their creaturehood. In this transgression, called the Original Sin, Adam and Eve reject their status as limited creatures. They choose themselves over God. They choose against their true identity as people made in the image and likeness of God, preferring their own rule over the Father's loving kindness. If the kingdom is about right relationship and communion with God, then to live under the loving dominion of the Creator is to acknowledge the truth about who God is and who we are. Through their choice to eat the fruit of the forbidden tree, Adam and Eve choose their own will over God's, refusing to acknowledge the reality of their dependence on God as his sons and daughters.

In doing so, they fall right into Satan's trap. In their desire to be free from God's rule and from any dependence on him, they reject his kingdom and make a kingdom out of their own will—a kingdom of Man. The tragedy of the Great Story is that Adam and Eve exchange the truth for a lie: desiring freedom, they fall into bondage and take all of creation with them.

EVERYTHING FALLS APART

Remember that God created humanity to experience love, and love cannot be coerced. It must be freely given. Therefore, God has given us free will—not so we can choose between good and evil, but rather so we can freely choose the good and embrace our identity as God's sons and daughters. When Adam and Eve, our first parents, choose disobedience instead of God's love, they do not use their free will, they *abuse* it.

This abuse has serious consequences that ripple across all of creation. The very first consequence is that the intimate bond between Adam and Eve ruptures: "Then the eyes of both of them were opened, and they knew that they were naked; so they sewed fig leaves together and made loincloths for themselves" (Genesis 3:7). Previously, our first parents were naked in the Garden of Eden and experienced no shame. Now, their bodies have become sources of temptation for each other, and they are ashamed. They create clothing to cover themselves, and this layer of protection creates a barrier that separates them.

The brokenness in the relationship between Adam and Eve possesses more than a physical dimension. Adam and Eve, who were spouses, helpmates, and partners with each other, find themselves at odds now. When the Lord confronts them after they eat the forbidden fruit, Adam blames both God **and** Eve: "The woman whom you put here with me—she gave me fruit from the tree, so I ate it" (Genesis 3:12). Adam wastes no time in shifting the blame to his wife, throwing her "under the bus" with a loud, *She did it!*

The rupture in communion between Adam and Eve, however difficult and tragic, is not the final consequence of their choice. Because of our first parents' disobedience, the intimate bond connecting humanity and God is ruptured as well. Adam and Eve's decision leads them to separate themselves from God. After the moment of the fall, God enters the garden and strolls through it. Adam and Eve, however, are nowhere to be found. They are hiding from God—a real rift has formed between them.

This is what is meant by the "stain of Original Sin." Since our first parents turned their backs on communion with God, all of their descendants—which is to say all of humanity (including you and me)—are born out of communion with God. This stain of Original Sin isn't a moral judgment on babies or a statement that all people are now evil. We are still made in the image of God, but that image has been wounded. Remember that God breathed his own Spirit (*ruah*) into them, giving them life, which was a share in his very life. Our first parents used that *breath*, the life God had given to them, to turn away from God. The stain of Original Sin is actually a lack: it is the absence of that divine life, which Adam and Eve lost for us by their disobedience.

Without that divine life, our intellect, will, emotions—all of the soul's faculties (or powers)—are wounded. Our bodies become sources of temptation, and we experience a hunger for God and his love that we often seek to fill with things that are not godly. Without that divine life, death enters the world, the final layer of separation introduced by Adam and Eve's sin. Even the original integrity of the human person— body and soul working together in harmony—breaks down as a result of sin. In God's plan, our bodies and souls would never separate, and we would dwell in the unity of God's love for all eternity. Now, the human body ages and breaks down, eventually succumbing to bodily death.

As if these weren't enough consequences, the whole created order is thrown into disarray:

To the woman he said: "I will intensify your toil in childbearing; / in pain you shall bring forth children. / Yet your urge shall be for your husband, / and he shall rule over you."

To the man he said: "Because you listened to your wife and ate from the tree about which I commanded you, You shall not eat from it,

"Cursed is the ground because of you! / In toil you shall eat its yield / all the days of your life. / Thorns and thistles it shall bear for you, / and you shall eat the grass of the field. / By the sweat of your brow you shall eat bread, / Until you return to the ground, / from which you were taken; / For you are dust, / and to dust you shall return" (Genesis 3:16-19).

Through the devil's lies, Adam and Eve abuse the gift of free will which God had given them, and their sin leaves all of creation wounded. Now tension, domination, lust, manipulation, and many other things threaten human relationships. Now natural disasters afflict the world. Now pain and illness enter the human experience—because of this moment. We sometimes look at the suffering of good people and want to blame God for it all. The truth is that evil and suffering and illness are real, but God had nothing to do with their coming into being. These evils have resulted from two things: the disobedience of our first parents and the seductive prompting of Satan.

God did not create evil, illness, and suffering—they come as a result of the fall of man. All of the suffering and illness and trauma that we experience in this life has its origin in this moment of the story. *If* God were truly a good God, and *if* he were truly all powerful, wouldn't he have fixed things for us? Many people have followed this train of thought and come to the conclusion that God cannot be all good or possess all power. Many therefore decide God does not exist, or that if he does, he's anything but loving.

The truth is that God could easily have erased the fall of man. He could have interrupted the story the moment Adam and Eve took a bite of the forbidden fruit, snapped his "fingers," and started Eden 2.0. Adam and Eve would be ushered offstage and Jose and Luana would take their place. Or, if God chose not to take this kind of cosmic mulligan, he could instantly have healed the effects of the Original Sin. Why didn't he? Well, this is where our story takes a wonderful twist.

God didn't reverse the fall of man or instantly heal its effects because he loves us too much.

On the surface, this may not make much sense. However, consider the reality that we are made in the image and likeness of the one who created us. God has a will that is free. If God made us in his image, we must also possess a free will. Love cannot be forced; it requires the free assent of the beloved. Therefore, God loves us too much simply to override the free choice of Adam and Eve—no matter how painful the results. If God simply declared a "do-over," his will would essentially take away the consequences of our free choices, rendering our will, in essence, not free. The Lord cherishes us too much to violate the gift of our free will.

All that being said, God would come off as a kind of cosmic monster if he simply left us in the midst of suffering, brokenness, and death—and that's where the story takes an amazing turn. God really does long to be in relationship with us, in an intimate bond. We do not have a distant God, far removed from the troubles of this life. God didn't wave a wand from his home in a distant place, nor did he save us as a kind of abstraction, a thought experiment that seemed like a good idea. Rather, this God who identified with his creation so much that he made us in his image comes after us.

We see that (again) in Genesis. From the first moment of Adam and Eve's disobedience, God seeks them. Eyes opened by their eating of the forbidden fruit, Adam and Eve hide from God out of shame. The Lord, strolling through the garden, knows that our first parents are now separated from him. "The Lord God then called to the man and asked him: Where are you?" (Genesis 3:9).

God, as a loving Father, cannot stand for his children to be separated from him. What Father could? What mother could? In essence, the Lord's children have run away, choosing to distance themselves from God's love. What parent of a runaway child wouldn't move heaven and earth for a chance at reunion? Therefore, from the moment Adam and Eve disobey him, God sets his plan for redemption and salvation—for reunion—in motion. The Lord not only calls after his children, but he goes in search of them.

THE INCARNATION

At last, the hero enters the story. He comes long after Adam and Eve and their children have died, "in the fullness of time" (Galatians 4:4), which means when God knew it should happen. Our hero comes without fanfare, not wearing golden armor or wielding a flaming sword, but in silence and in secret, born as an infant in a stable in a small backwater town of a conquered kingdom. God sends his Son, the Second Person of the Holy Trinity, to enter the human story, not as a king, but as a child of a poor family.

This quiet, poor birth of God's Son as a man is, perhaps, one of the most radical parts of the story, and the world almost missed it entirely. Yet throughout history the Lord was preparing his children for this radical moment. The events and truths of the Old Testament were a kind of preparation for this chapter of the story, foreshadowing what the Father planned to do for his children. To take just one example, consider this prophecy from the Old Testament book of the prophet Isaiah:

> Because of his anguish he shall see the light
>> because of his knowledge he shall be content:
> Therefore, I will give him his portion among the
>> many, and he shall divide the spoils with the mighty,
> Because he surrendered himself to death
>> was counted among the transgressors,
> Bore the sins of many,
>> and interceded for the transgressors.
>
> (Isaiah 53:11–12)

We hear this beautiful truth in the prologue of the Gospel of John: "And the Word became flesh / and made his dwelling among us" (1:14). The One who made us in his image took on our image to live as one of us. He incarnated—literally, became enfleshed. The Second Person of the Trinity, who is divine, took on our human nature. Out of his love for the Father and his compassion for us, the Son of God left the glory of heaven to live as one of us. This Jesus thought with a human mind, worked with human hands, cried human tears, and died a human death.[1]

In his earthly life and ministry, Jesus didn't simply announce the kingdom—he was the kingdom given flesh. Jesus Christ, the Son of God, embodies the kingdom. The reality of what we were created for, the life of communion with God and with one another, is not some fairy tale or theoretical abstraction. This kingdom of God is real and concrete. It

---

[1] Based on the Pastoral Constitution on the Church in the Modern World, *Gaudium et Spes*, 22.

looks like something ... or, rather, someone. That's why St. John Paul II wrote, in *Redemptoris Missio* ("Mission of the Redeemer"): "Since the 'Good News' is Christ, there is an identity between the message and the messenger, between saying, doing, and being. His power, the secret of the effectiveness of his actions, lies in his total identification with the message he announces; he proclaims the 'Good News' not just by what he says or does, but by what he is" (13).

What does living in communion with the Father look like? It looks like Jesus.

What do the freedom, wholeness, and integrity of the kingdom look like? They look like the life and person of Jesus.

What does it look like to love as the Father loves? It looks like Jesus.

Part of Jesus' mission is to reveal God's kingdom to us, and this revelation is not just given "from on high." Recall that in the Old Testament Book of Exodus, Moses went up the mountain of Sinai and there on the heights the Lord revealed his commandments. These Ten Commandments and the Mosaic laws that surrounded them were a revelation of what living as the people of God would look like. This revelation was given to one person out of the entire Israelite nation, and that person came down from the summit of Mount Sinai and delivered it to the people.

In Jesus Christ, the new revelation, which the Lord gives to all people, is quite different. A representative of the people does not climb to the heavens to receive it. Rather, God comes down among us, immerses himself in his people, and reveals the breadth and depth of kingdom life from within human experience. Because of this, the revelation extends not only to what kingdom life "is," but also to what it means to be human. In Jesus, God not only reveals himself to humanity, he also reveals to us the depth of our identity. In Jesus, we see the truth of what we were originally created for, the truth of who we are in the Father's eyes.

ONLY HUMAN

Often, after we have admitted to a mistake or failure, we say: "Well, what do you expect? After all, I'm *only* human." When we say that, we have accepted the woundedness, imperfection, and brokenness of our human nature as a *fait accompli*— as an unchangeable pillar of reality, as if that is all we could ever be. And when we do that, the Enemy smiles. Once Satan confuses us about the goodness and true identity of our Father, it's not difficult for him to weave a web of deception regarding our own identity. After all, if we were made by a God who is not good, or, even better, if we were made by some random biological process, then what value do we really have in the face of the vastness of the empty universe?

The person of Jesus, however, puts an end to that lie. We are not "only human." Our human nature may be wounded now, but that's not how we were originally created. What's more, in Jesus Christ, our human nature can be transformed, renewed, and restored. Therefore, at the heart of Christianity, at the heart of this Great Story of salvation, is an encounter with a person. It's not about rules and obligation and ritual. Although these things play an important role, without a relationship with the person at the heart of this story, they cannot bring about actual renewal and transformation. Again, St. John Paul II emphasized this when he wrote: "The kingdom of God is not a concept, a doctrine, or a program subject to free interpretation, but it is before all else a person with the face and name of Jesus of Nazareth, the image of the invisible God."[2]

This is how much our God cherishes us. He did not abandon us to the brokenness and suffering of the world after the fall, but rather sent his Son as one of us and transformed everything from inside the human condition. That is why one of the titles of Jesus is Emmanuel, "God with us."

So often our experience of living in a fallen and imperfect world lays burdens on us. Guilt that we feel for our own actions, or pain that we carry from the actions of others who have hurt us, can weigh us down. We also struggle with a sense of shame as we seek to come to terms with our mistakes and brokenness. There is a difference, however, between guilt and shame. Guilt says that I made a mistake, but shame says that I *am* a mistake—that there is something so fundamentally broken that I am not worth the love of another human person, let alone the love of God. Perhaps you have struggled with this at some point in your life. Maybe you are struggling with it now and you find it impossible to believe that God's radical choice to become like us has anything to do with you.

Yet this is the entire point of the Great Story. God's love for you is so profound that he came himself to make that love tangible in the brokenness and suffering of this world, so that in him there might be renewal, reunion, forgiveness,

---

[2] *Redemptoris Missio* ("Mission of the Redeemer"), 18.

and fullness. Your value goes beyond what you can produce. Your value is rooted in the Father's love for you, made clear in the person of Jesus.

You matter.

You.

Yes, you.

And the proof is that God himself became man for you.

There is another powerful prophecy (there are actually many) in the Old Testament Book of Isaiah. The Lord is speaking to Isaiah, telling him of the time of vindication for the people of Israel, a time when all suffering shall be turned to joy:

> Yet just as from the heavens
> > the rain and snow come down
> And do not return there
> > till they have watered the earth,
> > making it fertile and fruitful,
> Giving seed to the one who sows
> > and bread to the one who eats,
> So shall my word be
> > that goes forth from my mouth;
> It shall not return to me empty,
> > but shall do what pleases me,
> > achieving the end for which I sent it. (55:10–11)

Given the headlines we read every day in the news, it's pretty easy to think that God ignores our suffering, or that he remains silent and distant in the midst of what we are facing. The Great Story, however, calls us to a deeper truth: God is not silent in the face of the brokenness and hurt of this world.

He has spoken—definitively.

He has spoken a word, the Word, Jesus Christ. And that Word has not returned void or ineffective, but rather has achieved the end that God sent it to accomplish. In that Word, suffering has been transformed. In that Word, the Father's love is made manifest in the world.

Do we have ears to hear?

FURTHER REFLECTION

Take some time and prayerfully read through the first three chapters of the Genesis story. While this may sound strange, your goal isn't to read for comprehension. Sometimes we approach reading the Bible as if we were in a wrestling match with life-or-death stakes, and we try to power our way through it, either reading as quickly as possible to get it over with or agonizing over the meaning of every word or phrase.

Praying through these chapters in the Book of Genesis means neither rushing nor agonizing. As in the first chapter, you might find it helpful to pray for a few minutes before reading these Scriptures and ask the Lord specifically for the grace to receive exactly the message he is trying to communicate to you at this time in your life. Then, read the specific passage slowly and prayerfully several times. Take note of any words or phrases that jump out at you.

When you are finished reading the passage, ask the Lord to shed more light on the word(s) or passage that caught your attention. Ask God to reveal to you what, specifically, that word or phrase might have to do with your life right now.

SMALL GROUP QUESTIONS ─────────────────────

1. Thinking back on your life, have you ever had limitations placed upon you? What was that like? How did you react? Were the limitations reasonable or unreasonable?

2. Have you ever had the experience of losing a friendship or close relationship? Did you do anything to try and restore that relationship? What happened?

3. Looking at the person of Jesus, what are the three characteristics that he demonstrated in his earthly life that represent for you the most desirable or important elements of God's kingdom? Where have you experienced them in your own life?

4. The mystery of suffering in this world is often expressed in this question: Why do bad things happen to good people? How does the Genesis telling of the fall answer that question?

5. The conflict found in the Great Story is connected to every personal conflict we face in our lives. Share briefly about one major conflict you are encountering in your life right now. If Jesus is the Father's response to the great conflict of Original Sin, what would Jesus have to do with the conflict you just shared?

6. The reality that God enters the suffering of this world to transform it from the inside is often a new concept for

people. What does the reality that God became one of us mean to you?

7. If you have reflected on the Scripture passages in the Further Reflection section, what parts of the first three chapters of Genesis struck you or moved you when you read them?

CHAPTER 3

Jesus:
The Kingdom in Word and Deed

"The kingdom of God is at hand" (Mark 1:15).

Jesus, as the embodiment of the kingdom, reveals the love of the Father and the nature of God's kingdom through his every word and action. If God had not "taken on flesh" and lived among us, it would be easy to think of the kingdom as an abstraction or a nice tale to make us feel better as we muddle through our lives here on earth. With the Incarnation, however, heaven invades earth, and the kingdom breaks through into our broken world.

The reality of the kingdom is so central to the message of Jesus that the New Testament writers use the word "kingdom" 119 times. When Jesus sends out his disciples, he instructs them in this way: "Whatever town you enter and they welcome you, eat what is set before you, cure the sick in it and say to them, 'The kingdom of God is at hand for you'" (Luke 10:8–9).

Why does Jesus announce a kingdom? Remember that Original Sin, the disobedience of Adam and Eve, disrupted more than their inner life or psychology. Rather, it was a cosmic event that wounded all of creation. The kingdom of

God as announced by Jesus is, therefore, a dynamic restoration of creation—the breaking through of God's love, power, and sovereignty into created reality.

Right at the beginning of his ministry, Jesus stands up in a small synagogue in Nazareth and unrolls the scroll that contains the words of the prophet Isaiah. Remember that from the moment of the fall God was preparing the world for the coming of his Son. He sent the Israelite prophets, who not only spoke forth the mind and heart of God (which often led to their ridicule, exile, or worse), but also foretold the coming of the great Messiah, who would bring salvation and peace. Jesus reads from the section in which Isaiah describes how the Messiah will act: "The Spirit of the Lord is upon me, / because he has anointed me / to bring glad tidings to the poor. / He has sent me to proclaim liberty to captives / and recovery of sight to the blind, / to let the oppressed go free, / and to proclaim a year acceptable to the Lord" (Luke 4:18–19).

In fact, proclaiming a "year acceptable to the Lord" (a Jubilee Year) has its roots in the Old Testament. Every fifty years, on the Day of Atonement, the people of Israel would commence a Jubilee Year. During this holy year, prisoners could be released from their captivity and slaves could be freed. In addition, all debts were erased during a Jubilee Year (see Leviticus 25:10). According to Isaiah, the Messiah would usher in not just a Jubilee Year, but God's kingdom. The poor, the afflicted, those enslaved and oppressed would experience the richness of life, healing, and liberation.

In Luke's Gospel, when Jesus reads from the scrolls of Isaiah in the synagogue after being tempted in the desert, he is declaring the purpose of his ministry: bringing glad tidings to the poor, recovery of site to the blind, liberty to captives, and proclaiming a time acceptable to the Lord. Something is different in Jesus' proclamation. The previous Jubilees were finite; they lasted a single year and were repeated after a certain time frame. Now, however, the Father's plan is bearing real and lasting fruit in the person of Jesus. Therefore, the Jubilee that Christ proclaims is eternal, a lasting reign of peace and joy where justice, restoration, healing, and reconciliation triumph forever over the forces of decay, darkness, death, and sin. To the consternation of the Jewish leaders in Nazareth, Jesus publicly declares that he is the one about whom Isaiah had written. "Rolling up the scroll, he handed it back to the attendant and sat down, and the eyes of all in the synagogue looked intently at him. He said to them, 'Today this scripture passage is fulfilled in your hearing'" (Luke 4:20–21).

The kingdom announced by Jesus defies the expectations of the Jews. A conquered people, they long for salvation, but in their understanding this means a political and military leader who will overthrow Roman rule and establish the Jewish people as the center of geopolitical power. The whole arc of Jesus' life—and the thrust of his entire ministry—tells a different story. Born in a stable, living in a simple family, champion of the poor, critic of the Jewish religious leaders, preacher of forgiveness and mercy, this Jesus looks nothing like the Messiah they have been hoping for.

When the Jewish leaders eventually bring Jesus before Pilate, the Roman prefect who rules over the province of Judea, Jesus himself declares: "My kingdom does not belong to this world. If my kingdom did belong to this world, my attendants [would] be fighting to keep me from being handed over to the Jews. But as it is, my kingdom is not here" (John 18:36).

Earlier in his ministry Jesus declared: "The coming of the kingdom of God cannot be observed, and no one will announce, 'Look, here it is,' or, 'There it is.' For behold, the kingdom of God is *entos hymon*" (Luke 17:20–21). That is not a typo. *Entos hymon* is the untranslated Greek phrase that the Gospel writer Luke used in this section of his account of the life of Jesus. Many translations render this phrase as "within you." Coupled with Jesus' declaration that his kingdom is not of this world, the translation of the kingdom as being "within" has led many Christians to assume that God's kingdom is merely a kind of inner psychological event or subjective experience. A better translation of *entos hymon*, however, would be "among you." Read in this way, Jesus is not declaring an intangible, wispy, subjective kingdom. Rather, he makes a powerful statement equating himself with the kingdom.

In Luke's Gospel, the Pharisees ask Jesus when the kingdom of God will come. They are looking for a conquering Messiah who will perform great signs and send the Romans packing. Jesus proclaims something different—he is both the sign of the kingdom to come and the kingdom already present among them. The kingdom, therefore, although not rooted in earthly power, possesses flesh—an earthly significance.

Two major facets of Jesus' mission begin to unfold as he ministers and teaches: healing and forgiveness. St. John Paul II, when writing about Jesus' earthly ministry, pointed out, "Jesus' many healings ... signify that in the kingdom there will no longer be sickness or suffering, and that his mission, from the very beginning, is meant to free people from these evils."[3] Yet Jesus' healings are a sign of something even more

---

[3] *Redemptoris Missio* ("Mission of the Redeemer"), 14.

profound than physical restoration: he offers salvation and liberation from sin. Jesus understands that all the suffering and illness that exist in the world have their roots in Adam and Eve's disobedience—in Original Sin. Therefore, Jesus' many healings are a manifestation of kingdom reality—namely, that the Father's love is more powerful than sin and death. If God never intended for his creatures to experience blindness, and blindness has its roots in the fall, then opening the eyes of the blind also signifies a freedom from and triumph over the power of sin. That's why Jesus often says to those whom he heals, "Your faith has saved you" (Luke 18:42).

We see the liberating effects of the Father's power over sin in the story of the healing of the paralytic man (see Luke 5:17–26). Jesus is teaching in a village, and some men lower a paralyzed man on a mat through the roof because there are so many people crowded around Jesus that they can't get their friend near him. Moved by their faith, Jesus turns to the paralyzed man and forgives his sins. What follows next is the kingdom in action:

> Then the scribes and Pharisees began to ask them-
> selves, "Who is this who speaks blasphemies? Who
> but God alone can forgive sins?" Jesus knew their
> thoughts and said to them in reply, "What are you
> thinking in your hearts? Which is easier, to say, 'Your
> sins are forgiven,' or to say, 'Rise and walk?' But that
> you may know that the Son of Man has author-
> ity on earth to forgive sins"—he said to the man
> who was paralyzed, "I say to you, rise, pick up your
> stretcher, and go home." He stood up immediately
> before them, picked up what he had been lying on,

and went home, glorifying God. Then astonishment
seized them all and they glorified God, and, struck
with awe, they said, "We have seen incredible things
today." (Luke 5:21–26)

This manifestation of the Father's power over sin awak-
ens faith in those who witness it. Time and time again in
the four Gospels we see Jesus' healings stirring hearts toward
conversion and really inviting those who encounter Jesus
to a new perspective. Sometimes his healings challenge the
worldviews of those around him. They raise the question of
Jesus' identity and divinity—like in the story above, as the
Pharisees wrestle with Jesus' claim to forgive sins in light
of the healing of the paralyzed man. Jesus' healings become
signs of the truth he proclaims.

Jesus also proclaims the reality of the kingdom in words
to those who will listen. In his many parables and teachings, he describes the characteristics of kingdom life. In fact,
through Jesus' ministry, we see that the kingdom is about
multiplication, generation, new life, forgiveness, mercy, communion, and relationship with the Father. Kingdom life has
radically different principles than the ones you and I have
learned growing up in this fallen world. In the kingdom, the
last shall be first (see Matthew 20:16), the one who tries to
save his life will lose it (Luke 9:24), those who have much
will receive even more (Matthew 13:12). Unlike the world's
economy, driven by scarcity and the reality of demand, the
economy of the kingdom is founded on abundance, fruitful-
ness, availability, and love. In the kingdom, God's love, mercy,
and justice spill into creation, changing and transforming all
things. In truth, the kingdom impacts individuals, families,

relationships, culture, business, economics, sociological categories, race relations, and the earth itself.

Love, as we have mentioned, always seeks the beloved. Love is dynamic and creative, and it pours itself out for others. God's desire is that we should experience the reality of that abundant love, freedom, joy, restoration, and mercy *in this life*, and not merely as a prize in the next life if we behave well in this one. That's why Jesus declares, "I came so that they might have life and have it more abundantly" (John 10:10). This abundant life is kingdom life. Ultimately, it touches every facet of creation because the One who created everything, our heavenly Father, does not stand idly by and allow us to suffer under the weight of sin, brokenness, and death. Through the Incarnation and the life, ministry, and work of his Son, the Father restores what has been lost.

Do we really believe that? Perhaps the reality of suffering in the world keeps us from accepting God's love. Maybe our own sufferings have caused us to doubt that he cares for us. After all, Jesus is supposed to have proclaimed God's kingdom and made it present to us, so why is there so much suffering still? The reality is that the kingdom of God has burst forth among us through Jesus' life and ministry. The kingdom is present here on earth now, but it is not yet fully manifest. There's more to the story.

Beyond the question of suffering, many of us have difficulties or obstacles in our lives that hold us back from taking Jesus at his word. What hurts have you been carrying with you for too long? What obstacles keep you from experiencing love and believing in the Father's love for you? How would your life be different if these obstacles and wounds could be bound up and healed?

In the New Testament, anyone who encounters Jesus with an open heart always receives something. The Lord's promise of new life in the kingdom is a sure promise, and he desires to encounter each of us today. Wherever Jesus is proclaimed and made present today, healing and restoration abound. Brokenness, shame, sin—none of it is a match for the power of the Lord. As we open ourselves more and more to this life that Jesus offers us, we will find ourselves becoming more free, experiencing authentic healing, and drawing closer to the Father's heart.

Make no mistake—the kingdom of God is here.

And it is here for you.

FURTHER REFLECTION

Take some time (at least fifteen minutes a day for the next few days) and prayerfully read through the following stories from the Gospels:

- Luke 5:17–26

- Luke 18:35–43

- John 4:4–42

- John 9:1–41

After you have read through them a few times, read them again, and this time try to imagine yourself in that reading. Picture yourself in the scene as the author describes it. Notice what you see, smell, and hear. You can do this either by yourself or in a group—with one person reading while the others go through this imaginative exercise. When you are done, take a moment to write down (or share with one another) what you experienced, who you were in the story, and how you felt as that person as the story unfolded.

1. Are you aware of having encountered God's healing power in your own life? Can you pinpoint areas where that healing had a ripple effect in your life and in the lives of those around you?

2. All of us, like the Jewish leaders of Jesus' time, are tempted to look for a savior who will rid our lives of the circumstances and people we don't like. Where might God be inviting you to a transformation through personal conversion? Can you name one area where God is asking you to change—and then invite him in to set you free?

3. If you encountered Jesus standing right in front of you today, what would you ask of him?

4. Where do you think God could be inviting you to a fuller participation in kingdom life? What negative thought pattern, prejudice, or grudge can you hand over? What person in your life might need your forgiveness?

5. How can you trust God and take him at his word when you or someone you love is experiencing suffering?

6. What if Jesus really did mean the things that he said about abundant life, mercy, forgiveness, and peace? What would happen if your heart were opened even more to the transforming power of God's love? How would your life be different?

CHAPTER 4

Jesus Embraces the Cross

The kingdom of God has enemies.

On the surface, that may seem surprising. After all, who would oppose peace, fulfillment, joy, abundance, and the many amazing things God's love offers? Yet, beginning with Satan and his minions who rebelled against God, and continuing with Adam and Eve's disobedience, this is precisely what God's creatures do.

Ever since the fall, we experience a disconnect between what we know we should do and what we actually do. Rather than wanting what God wants, we set our desires above his, putting ourselves in his place. The reality of the kingdom now poses a serious threat. After all, to one who has spent all his effort in amassing a great deal of earthly wealth, social standing, or authority, a kingdom where the last shall be first and the mighty will be cast down in favor of the lowly (see Luke 1:46–55) is not something to look forward to.

In his earthly ministry Jesus very clearly challenges the political, cultural, and moral systems of his day. He breaks religious laws by healing on the Sabbath, a traditional day of rest where no work could be done; he allies himself with the poor, the unclean, and the outcast; he calls out the hypocrisy of Jewish religious and moral leaders; and he declares himself God, a blasphemous act punishable by death. Jesus' words and actions provoke confrontation with religious and political authorities, and these authorities eventually conspire to capture, punish, and kill him.

It would be a mistake, however, simply to see Jesus as a political or social revolutionary, a kind of martyr put to death for a cause. As this chapter of the story unfolds, and we see Jesus imprisoned, tortured, and, ultimately, crucified, it is crucial that we recognize the deeper current underneath the narrative. Jesus does not get swept up and carried to the cross as a consequence of a revolutionary lifestyle. He isn't a powerless and passive figure whose bad luck and lack of diplomacy lead him in over his head. Rather, he is the Son of God who embraces death. The One through whom all was created (see John 1:3; Colossians 1:16) freely offers his life. In the Gospel of John he tells his followers: "This is why the Father loves me, because I lay down my life in order to take it up again. No one takes it from me, but I lay it down on my own. I have power to lay it down, and power to take it up again" (10:17–18).

Something far deeper than mere political martyrdom is happening in this chapter of the story, something related to the mission of Jesus Christ. The Father sends the Son into the world to accomplish something tangible. In fact, the Father doesn't just *send* the Son; he *gives* the Son to the world: "For God so loved the world that he gave his only Son, so that everyone who believes in him might not perish but might have eternal life" (John 3:16). The Father makes a gift of the Son for the world, and the Son, out of love and fidelity to the Father, embraces the mission and makes himself an offering for the world.

But why?

Why would the Son of God, the king of kings, embrace one of the most humiliating deaths—the death of a common criminal? And what would such a death accomplish? To unravel the mystery behind this chapter of our story, we have to look deeper into history. The answers just might prove life-changing.

LET'S MAKE A DEAL

Deep in the primal instincts of humanity is an understanding of the power of sacrifice. Ancient peoples, tribes, and nations sometimes sacrificed the first fruits of the field, the first wine or alcohol from the fermentation process, and especially animals as an offering to the gods, spirits, or other elemental forces that they believed governed their lives. These offerings were meant to appease, please, cajole, divine the best future action, seal a bargain, or do any number of other things to move the powers that govern the world.

The Old Testament concept of covenant emerged out of this sacrificial worldview. In our modern understanding, a covenant is a kind of agreement or contract between two parties. In the Old Testament, a covenant was much more. Far more than simply an agreement between two parties, a covenant was more like an exchange of persons, a declaration that "I will be for you" and "you will be for me." One example of covenant that still exists in our society is marriage, an exchange of consent that the spouses now will live for each other.

Entering into a covenant in the period of the Old Testament was serious business that required the sacrifice of an animal. Covenantal practices included not only the killing of an animal (like a ram or bull), but cutting that animal in two. The parties entering into a particular covenant would walk between the sides of the animal with the understanding that if they broke that covenant, they would bring upon themselves a curse that would tear their lives as the animal they walked between had been torn. This kind of animal sacrifice was so central to the reality of covenants that the Hebrew phrase "to make a covenant," *kārat berît*, literally translates as "to cut a covenant."

Looking back through the Old Testament, we see God declaring his love for the Israelites by entering into covenants with them. Time and time again, the Lord approaches the Israelites and binds himself to them. Noah, Abraham, Moses, and David, for example, all entered into covenants with God on behalf of the Israelites. We see the intimate, fierce love that God has for his people throughout the Old Testament in the nuptial language that he frequently uses. The prophet Jeremiah, speaking a word of comfort and a prophecy of restoration to the Israelites, reflects this covenantal and nuptial imagery: "Go, cry out this message for Jerusalem to hear! / I remember the devotion of your youth, / how you loved me as a bride, / Following me in the wilderness, / in a land unsown" (Jeremiah 2:2).

Sadly, Israel acted, time and again, as an unfaithful bride to the Lord, her Bridegroom. The Old Testament recounts Israel's continued infidelity: turning from the commands and the law of the Lord, worshiping foreign gods, and forsaking the love of the One who delivered her out of slavery in Egypt. Yet the history of the Israelites is really a testament to the faithfulness of God, who calls his people back repeatedly.

Every time they violate the covenant, he renews it. With each covenant, we see the tenacious love of God unwilling to let his beloved go, unwilling to allow his creatures to suffer the consequences of their abuse of free will.

As each successive covenant unfolds, a promise develops, hidden at first, hinted at and foreshadowed, and then prophesied to the whole of Israel—a promise of a new covenant, a deeper, more intimate relationship between God and His people. In the Book of Jeremiah we read:

> See, days are coming—oracle of the LORD—when I will make a new covenant with the house of Israel and the house of Judah. It will not be like the covenant I made with their ancestors the day I took them by the hand to lead them out of the land of Egypt. They broke my covenant, though I was their master—oracle of the LORD. But this is the covenant I will make with the house of Israel after those days—oracle of the LORD. I will place my law within them, and write it upon their hearts; I will be their God, and they shall be my people. They will no longer teach their friends and relatives, "Know the LORD!" Everyone, from least to greatest, shall know me—oracle of the LORD—for I will forgive their iniquity and no longer remember their sin. (31:31–34)

In fact, the covenants with Israel were God's way of preparing the world for the new and final covenant in Jesus Christ. Like a gentle and patient Father, the Lord never forces his will upon his people, but constantly invites them back into relationship. Knowing from the moment of humanity's first rebellion that he would make a way, the Father prepared the "soil" of the world so that it could receive the seed of the Gospel. God's plan of salvation always included the coming of his Son.

Consider the Israelites' escape from slavery in Egypt, detailed in the Old Testament Book of Exodus. The Lord God called on Moses to be his representative to Pharaoh. Moses shared God's command with the ruler of Egypt: "Let my people go." But Pharaoh refused. As a result, God visited plague after plague on the nation of Egypt, but Pharaoh's heart remained hardened. So, God planned to visit a final, devastating plague on Egypt: the firstborn male of every species would die. To ensure the Angel of Death spared the Israelites, God gave his people instructions through Moses:

Tell the whole community of Israel: On the tenth of this month every family must procure for itself a lamb, one apiece for each household. If a household is too small for a lamb, it along with its nearest neighbor will procure one, and apportion the lamb's cost in proportion to the number of persons, according to what each household consumes. Your lamb must be a year-old male and without blemish. You may take it from either the sheep or the goats. You will keep it until the fourteenth day of this month, and then, with the whole community of Israel assembled, it will be slaughtered during the evening twilight. They will take some of its blood and apply it to the two doorposts and the lintel of the houses in which they eat it....

For on this same night I will go through Egypt, strik-
ing down every firstborn in the land, human being
and beast alike, and executing judgment on all the
gods of Egypt—I, the LORD! But for you the blood
will mark the houses where you are. Seeing the
blood, I will pass over you; thereby, when I strike the
land of Egypt, no destructive blow will come upon
you. (Exodus 12:3–13)

The Israelites were spared punishment and death through
the sacrifice of a spotless, perfect lamb. Now, God could have
saved the Israelites in any number of ways. Yet he chose to
use the sacrifice of a pure lamb as a means of sparing his
people. Again, there is a deeper purpose here. The Lord was
preparing the world to receive the saving work of Christ on
the cross.

The meaning is clear.

The coming of Jesus—his incarnation, life, and especially
his death—fulfill the promises that God made to his people.
For creation to experience the Father's saving love, there
must be a covenant enacted by God, a divine invitation. Jesus,
the Word of God made flesh, is a divine person with a divine
nature. Through his "yes" to the Father's plan, the covenant
is proposed by God to creation. Jesus stands in the Father's
place to offer the covenant. Because he is also our brother, a
human being just like us but without sin, Jesus stands in for
all humanity as our faithful representative in the covenant.

The problem with covenants, as we have seen, has never
been with God, but with our response. Often faithless and
fickle, with our wounded and compromised intellect, will,

and emotions, we cannot keep up our end of the covenant. Jesus, who also possesses a human nature, "has similarly been tested in every way, yet without sin" (Hebrews 4:15). Jesus lives out his earthly life in perfect obedience to the Father's will.

Covenants require a worthy sacrifice in order to be sealed. In the old covenants God made with his people, the Mosaic Law provided remedies for those who fell short of the Law or broke it in some way. Touching an unclean person, for example, would render one unclean and therefore outcast from society. Ritual purification rendered one externally clean and restored that person to the community. Atonement worked in a similar way. To make satisfaction for sinning, individuals could purchase animals, which were then sacrificed at the Temple in Jerusalem by a priest. These sacrifices and purification rituals dealt with one's external relationship with God and the community. However, they had no power to change the heart or transform the inner person—thus they needed to be repeated over and over again.

With the coming of Jesus, the cycle of imperfect sacrifices comes to an end. Not only does Jesus represent both God and man in this new covenant, but as he embraces his death on the cross he becomes the sacrifice that seals the covenant. The new covenant in Jesus Christ is "cut" (*kārat berît*) with his torn flesh and the spilling of his blood. Jesus is both God and man, priest and victim in this covenant, sealed by a sacrifice that never needs to be repeated because Jesus is the eternal Son of God. St. Peter reminds us: "Realizing that you were ransomed from your futile conduct, handed on by your ancestors, not with perishable things like silver or gold but with the precious blood of Christ as of a spotless unblemished lamb. He was known before the foundation of the world but revealed in the final time for you" (1 Peter 1:18–20).

Just as the Israelites escaped the punishment of death and the slavery of Egypt through the sacrifice of unblemished lambs, you and I—and all of creation—have a way back to the Father that flows from the blood of the spotless Lamb of God, Jesus, who threw his arms around the cross … all the while seeing your face.

HOW MUCH DOES GOD LOVE ME?

When I was about ten years old, I fell in love with a girl from my grade school—I'll call her Susan (not her real name) to avoid any potential embarrassment. I thought the sun rose and set wherever Susan went. My little heart went aflutter whenever she was around. One summer day I took my bicycle and rode it to the local park in my town. There, I caught sight of Susan, who happened to be drinking from a water fountain. This was it, I thought—this was my moment to let Susan know how I felt about her. I stopped my bike and desperately tried to think of some way to announce my love for her. Being ten years old, and something of an awkward kid, I found myself unable to come up with anything—until inspiration struck! Earlier in the day it had rained, and the park grounds were rapidly drying, leaving small clumps of mud in places where the earth was turned up. I knew in that moment that if I picked up a clump of mud and threw it with all my might at Susan, she would know just how I felt.

And that's exactly what I did.

Now, I didn't end up dating anyone until I was seventeen, and to this day I'm still not sure if there is a connection between my experience with Susan and that fact. One thing I do know clearly, however: God is a far better communicator of his love than I am. That's exactly what the cross is—a declaration of God's love and mercy for you, me, and all of the world. We might look at the cross, with its brutality and violence, and somehow see God's condemnation of the world, his judgment and wrath. But the good news of this story is that in Jesus, God's justice and mercy meet. The Bible tells us clearly that "God did not send his Son into the world to condemn the world, but that the world might be saved through him" (John 3:17).

Do you want to know how much you are loved and cherished by the Lord of the universe? Do you want to know how much your life is worth—right now, not in some future state when you have finally conquered all of your faults and are living a "perfect" life?

The answer is simple.

You are worth the very life of God.

That is how much the Father values you. Not for what you have done, but simply for who you are. Sometimes we try to impress God with our actions, as if we can somehow earn God's love or convince him to love us even more. The truth is, you can't do anything to make God love you anymore than he already does right now. Nothing that you have done (or ever will do) can change the truth about God's love for you. You have always been worth the very life of his Son. Even if you were the only person who ever lived on the earth, Jesus would still have embraced the cross for you.

WHAT REALLY HAPPENED
ON THE CROSS?

The sacrifice of Jesus on the cross did more than just seal the new covenant. Through his death, Jesus opened the way back to the Father's love, restoring all of creation to the kingdom. This is the radical power of the story of Jesus, and this chapter of the story is literally the crux, the turning point of the entire narrative. Up until now, things have fallen apart. The enemy struck his blow in the Garden of Eden, and Adam and Eve abused their free will, sending the entire cosmos into a tailspin. Separated from God and mastered by the powers of sin and death, humanity struggled for thousands of years. In the midst of this brokenness, the Father kept seeding the world with the message of his love, preparing and pruning it carefully, like a master gardener working across the centuries, preparing his creation for the breaking forth of his kingdom once again. All of these plans came to fulfillment in the birth, life, ministry, passion, and death of Jesus.

Many of us have heard this part of the story repeated throughout our lives, without ever having a clear sense of what really happened on the cross. How does Christ's death on the cross restore us to the Father's love? What about his death makes it effective? How did his sacrifice accomplish our salvation? Once again, we have to go back and look at the Israelites. As part of the law given them by the Lord through Moses, the Israelites were commanded to celebrate a Day of Atonement. On that day, the high priest would take two goats. He would slaughter one and use its blood to cleanse the Tent of Meeting (the tent of God's presence, which traveled with the Israelites). Then he would ritually place all of the people's sins upon the head of the other goat, and the people would drive that goat into the wilderness, carrying the people's sins away with it. This goat was called the scapegoat. This ritual, found in the Old Testament Book of Leviticus, points clearly to the suffering and death of Jesus.

Another prophecy, taken from Isaiah and written many hundreds of years after the Book of Leviticus, speaks even more clearly of the Father's plan to send someone to save his people and bear their burdens:

> My servant, the just one, shall justify the many,
>   their iniquity he shall bear.
> Therefore I will give him his portion among the many,
>   and he shall divide the spoils with the mighty,
> Because he surrendered himself to death,
>   was counted among the transgressors;
> Bore the sins of many,
>   and interceded for the transgressors.
>
> (Isaiah 53:11–12)

Jesus bears on himself the brokenness, sin, and guilt of the world. As the apostle Paul wrote in his Second Letter to the Corinthians: "For our sake he made him to be sin who did not know sin, so that we might become the righteousness of God in him" (5:21). Jesus embraces his death on the cross to become our scapegoat. The sinfulness of the world is placed upon him, and like the scapegoat of Leviticus, he is exiled, seen as unclean, and despised by the community whose sins he takes upon his shoulders.

But what does it mean to bear the sin of another? Remember in the opening chapter of the story, Adam and Eve turned their backs on God, committing the first sin. From that part of our story, we can see that sin ruptures our relationship with God. Because God is infinitely good, holy, and loving, he deserves our praise, worship, and obedience. When we sin, we commit an offense against a perfect and infinite God. We also sin against a God who is pure justice. It might help to explore for a moment what we mean by God's justice. From a purely human perspective, we often define justice as giving someone their due or what they deserve. God's justice is far deeper—and woven into the very fabric of creation. The word "justice" comes from the Latin word *iustitia*, which can mean "right order." The justice of God, then, involves the right ordering and right relationships between everything in creation. All other forms of justice, including the right ordering of relationships between individuals within (and between) communities—what we call social justice—depends on the justice of God. Sin, then, is an act that breaks that right order. The justice of God demands satisfaction, not because God is petty, or because his feelings are hurt. Rather, the very nature of God's justice requires this wound in right order to be healed, or atoned for. If God ignored the demands of justice, he wouldn't be perfect justice.

Therefore, sin is an offense that must be atoned for, not because God is insecure, harsh, or vindictive. Rather, the nature of sin is incompatible with the nature of God, leading to separation from God unless that sin is dealt with. Because God is infinite and eternal goodness, sinning against him has eternal consequences. You and I, however, are finite people. On our own, apart from something or someone who is infinite, nothing we do—no amount of good deeds, or prayers, or chanting, or devotions—will ever make satisfaction for the offenses God has received.

We simply can't do it.

And here's where the story gets really good. The truth is that since justice and mercy are part of God's nature, they can never be separated from each other. We could never make up for the world's transgressions against God, so God—out of his goodness and mercy—finds a way for us. He doesn't leave us to sit in our condemnation and punishment (no matter how just). He sends his own Son to make satisfaction for that offense. In Jesus, God's perfect justice and his perfect mercy meet. Jesus, because he is God, is infinite in goodness, justice, love, and mercy. Because he is fully human, he has the power to atone for the sins committed by human beings. Thus Jesus embraces his death on the cross for us.

Let's put it a slightly different way. Say you and I are children at a store filled with expensive merchandise, and the store has signs that clearly say, "Do not play ball." We decide, however, that it would be a lot of fun to play catch in the aisles of the store. We run around and chuck this ball at each other. Soon, we damage an item in that store. In addition to our parents' anger, we also have to make restitution for what we broke. However, that item costs more money than we will ever make in a lifetime of recycling cans, selling lemonade, or saving up chore money. Since we can't pay that price, we're stuck with a broken item, and we probably will never be allowed to step foot in the store again.

But what would happen if the owner of the store saw how upset we were and out of compassion for us wanted to help? He couldn't just ignore that broken item and pretend like it was still whole. He has a very expensive debt that he can't make up (because he can no longer sell the item). It will stay on his books until he takes some kind of financial hit for it. So, instead of ignoring it, he decides to open his own wallet and pay for it personally. Of course, this analogy "limps" a bit—all analogies do. But in a way, this is what Jesus has done for us. Through his sacrifice, the price for our brokenness is paid in full. When it comes to our salvation, Jesus pays the price for us, satisfying the demands of justice and revealing the depths of God's mercy and love.

THE PRICE OF JUSTICE

The story of Jesus is a love story; it is a tale of the boundless and eternal love that God holds for us. It would be easy to hear the phrase "Jesus satisfied the demands of God's justice" and conclude, first of all, that the Father is some vengeful figure rubbing his hands together in glee during the beating, torture, and crucifixion of Jesus. We could even conclude that the whole process of Jesus' suffering and death functions like some kind of impersonal transaction. However, it is love that holds the key to unlocking the central meaning of this chapter in the story, the love between the Father and the Son. Jesus' death on the cross doesn't stem from the Father desiring to punish someone. Rather, Jesus' experience on the cross stems from sin's very nature, the consequences of which Jesus took upon himself because of love. In a very real sense, therefore, Jesus not only satisfies the demands of God's justice, but also of God's love.

The Father loved the Son before all time, and the Son loved the Father from all eternity. Their relationship has always been. This connection or communion between Father and Son did not cease to exist during the earthly life of Jesus Christ. Throughout his life and ministry Jesus would take time daily to pray. He would speak openly of the Father's love, and he would say startling things like: "The Father and I are one" (John 10:30), or the "son cannot do anything on his own, but only what he sees his father doing" (John 5:19), or "whoever has seen me has seen the Father" (John 14:9).

Cardinal Joseph Ratzinger, before he was elected Pope Benedict XVI, wrote about this radical connection between Jesus and the Father. He saw how the reality of "sonship" shaped the life of Jesus Christ: "'Son' is a basic confession in the sense that it provides the key to interpretation, making everything else [about Jesus' life] accessible and intelligible."[4] For Ratzinger, the testimony of the New Testament is, essentially, the playing out of this intimate communion: "For the entire Gospel testimony is unanimous that Jesus' words and deeds flowed from his most intimate communion with the Father ... the essential events of Jesus' activity proceeded from the core of his personality and that this core was his dialogue with the Father."[5]

Far from being a distant and cruel deity demanding justice, God knew intimately what it would cost to bring his children back to him. The price of restoring all of creation would be the very life of his beloved Son. Recall that at the moment of his baptism in the Jordan River Jesus received the affirmation of his Father. God split the heavens, the Holy

---

[4] Joseph Ratzinger, "Taking Bearings in Christology," in *Behold the Pierced One* (San Francisco: Ignatius Press, 1986), 17.

[5] Ibid., 17-18.

Spirit descended in the form of a dove, and "a voice came from heaven, 'You are my beloved Son; with you I am well pleased'" (Luke 3:22). In fact, the Father has demonstrated unimaginable love for us by sending his Son, knowing that Jesus would suffer humiliation, torture, and death.

Nor did Jesus say "yes" casually to the Father's plan. Jesus was not simply a divine person wearing a human disguise. He was both true God and true man—he was like us in all things except giving in to temptation and sinning. Therefore, his death would be physically, emotionally, and psychologically painful. To allow himself to become both a sin offering and the seal of the new covenant with God the Father would cost Jesus great suffering. It would bring his earthly life to an abrupt and horrible end. If we look more deeply at the process of his suffering and death, however, we see that something far more costly than human pain and death occurs.

After Jesus celebrates a Passover meal with his disciples in Jerusalem, he takes some of them with him to the Garden of Gethsemane. There, he instructs them to pray and remain with him while he prays to the Father. In fact, in the Gospel of Mark, Jesus says something curious to his disciples: "My soul is sorrowful even to death. Remain here and keep watch" (14:34). This part of the story is traditionally called the Agony in the Garden.

For decades, what Jesus says to his disciples in the garden puzzled me greatly. I understood that Jesus saw the death that was waiting for him in Jerusalem, and I could certainly see how that would be troubling to a person. He was no normal person, however. This was *Jesus*—the one who raised the dead, calmed storms, walked on water, cast out demons, and claimed not just intimacy but equality with the Father. How does Jesus experience sorrow in his soul if he truly was who he claimed to be?

Thinking through this, there are probably several other possible reasons for Jesus to suffer this agony in the Garden of Gethsemane. He is incredibly sad that one of his closest friends has betrayed him. He knows many people will never accept the reconciliation his death will bring about. He is horrified at the evil that will be done in his name in the future. In his human nature, he probably doubts the success of his mission, and he worries about whether the Father will rescue him from death: "Abba, Father, all things are possible to you. Take this cup away from me, but not what I will but what you will" (Mark 14:36). Yet all of these horrors pale before the ultimate cause of Jesus' agony and suffering.

The cup that Jesus sees before him, the cup he begs the Father to take away from him, symbolizes his sacrifice. Though he doesn't want to drink from the cup, Jesus pledges his faithfulness to the Father's plan. The question remains what, ultimately, does this cup hold? Is it sin? Suffering? Blood? Is it Jesus' death? The answer to this question might surprise you.

Remember that sin is incompatible with the very nature of God. Nothing that is imperfect or sinful can stand in his presence. That's why the apostle Paul wrote that "the wages of sin is death" (Romans 6:23), as sin separates us from God. And while God loves us even when we sin, in his great love he despises what sin has made us become. If that sounds harsh, think of what might happen if you had children and one of them started using drugs until she became addicted. Now, you would love your daughter in spite of what she might have done trying to feed her habit—yet you would probably be angry at *what your daughter has become* because of the drugs! That anger doesn't negate your love. In fact, that anger is a strong proof of your love, because you see how this terrible habit is destroying the person you care about so deeply.

In the same way, God abhors what sin does to each of us, and the separation from him that it causes. So, what is in the cup that Jesus begs the Father to take away from him? Theologian Father Thomas Weinandy writes in his book *Jesus the Christ*: "In the Garden of Gethsemane, it was this cup of condemnation [due to sin] that the Son, in agony, saw set before him in its full horror."[6] Sin provokes God's just wrath, and, according to Father Weinandy, this wrath is "simply God's approval of what sin itself rightfully demands."[7] Therefore, "it is the wrath of God in this sense, as the ultimate necessary consequence of the playing out of sin in the presence of the good and holy, that the son of God experienced."[8] In the Garden of Gethsemane, Jesus accepts God's wrath for himself. He accepts it not because he deserves it, but out of his incredible love for us.

The ultimate necessary consequence of sin, as we have explored, is separation from God. Thus the agony that Jesus suffers is first and foremost a rupturing of his intimate communion with the Father—a separation and abandonment by God. This Jesus, whose whole life is characterized by communion with the Father, whose very identity rests on the reality of his sonship in relation to the Father, now begins to experience the horror of separation from the Father.

---

[6] Thomas G. Weinandy, OFM Cap, *Jesus the Christ* (Huntington, IN: Our Sunday Visitor), 108.

[7] Ibid., 109.

[8] Ibid.

We tend to think of agony as the suffering of intense physical or mental pain, or perhaps a surge of negative emotion. In the first century, when the stories of Jesus were being collected and written, *agonia* (the Greek word from which we derive "agony" in English) also held a technical meaning. It referred to the sweat that athletes produced as they warmed up for their competitive events. In the Olympics, for example, spectators gathered to watch a wrestler's *agonia*. This warm-up was seen as connected to the main event. As a wrestler rubbed oil on his body, limbered up, and ran through practice drills with a partner, it wasn't just in anticipation of what would come, it was already part of the competitive event. In this sense, then, Jesus' agony in the garden wasn't simply an anticipation of the suffering to come, but rather a real and present part of his passion, which would culminate with his death on the cross the following morning.

Here the Great Story comes full circle. God, as the master storyteller, weaves together profound themes throughout human history, and nowhere is this more apparent than in Jesus' passion. The fall of man took place in a garden (Eden) around a tree (the Tree of the Knowledge of Good and Evil), and now the salvation of man begins in a garden (Gethsemane) and will be completed on a tree (the wood of the cross). What follows after the agony in the garden—Jesus' arrest, interrogation at the hands of religious and political leaders, torture, crucifixion, and death—are all parts of one single event.

By freely accepting the cup from his Father's hands, Jesus takes on himself the punishment that we deserve: separation from the One who created us for love. In his person, the Son experiences the abandonment that the rest of us deserve for our sins. We see the culmination of his suffering on the cross.

Jesus, bloodied and bruised from cruel whipping and torture, hanging from the cross as the weight of his body slowly crushes his lungs, cries out, "My God, my God, why have you forsaken me?" (Matthew 27:46). The communion between the Father and the Son, though never completely broken, is stretched to its breaking point.

After hours hanging on the cross, Jesus asks for a drink. Upon receiving a little bit of wine soaked on a sponge, he looks up to heaven and says, "It is finished" (John 19:30). Then, he gives up his spirit and dies. With Jesus' death, the sacrifice has been fully offered. He has paid the price for you and me, restoring us to right relationship and freeing us from the power of sin. What does that mean? It means that there is no injustice, no brokenness, no sin that can ever hold us in bondage again if we allow the love of God, demonstrated on the cross, to penetrate our lives. It means that this one act of love has changed everything for us. Our joys are amplified and our sorrows can be transformed. It means that no matter what we may struggle with in our lives—shame, addiction, negative self-image, anger, eating disorders, abuse, or anything else—nothing is stronger than the power of Christ's sacrifice on the cross.

Why does the Son willingly embrace this unspeakable suffering? There is only one reason: his incredible love for us. Jesus has become an offering, a scapegoat, for the sinfulness of the world. Despised, rejected, tortured, abandoned, and killed—not for nameless and faceless people, but for you and me. The punishment that you and I deserve, the loss of friendship with God and kingdom life, Jesus takes upon himself.

Indeed, we have been bought. There is a claim now upon our lives. Without the cross, you and I would forever bow before the weight of our own brokenness, the chains of our compulsions and addictions, the horror of the grief and sorrow and futility of life. Yet in his love for you, Jesus has carried the weight of the cross and willingly suffered death.

As he gazed heavenward and cried out to his heavenly Father, Jesus saw your face and your life.

The cross has made a way—and that's not even the end of our story!

FURTHER REFLECTION

Take some time (at least fifteen minutes a day) and prayerfully read through the Passion Narrative found in the Gospel of John (18:1 through 19:42). Again, your goal isn't to read for comprehension. Praying through these chapters means neither rushing nor agonizing. As in the first chapter, you might find it helpful to pray for a few minutes before reading these Scriptures and ask the Lord specifically for the grace to receive exactly the message he wants to communicate to you at this time in your life. Then, read the specific passage slowly and prayerfully several times. Take note of any words or phrases that jump out at you.

When you are finished reading the passage, ask the Lord to shed more light on the word(s) or passage that jumped out at you. Ask God to reveal to you what, specifically, that word or phrase might have to do with your life right now.

After you have read through this narrative several times, read it again, and this time try and imagine yourself in that reading. In other words, picture yourself in the scene as the author describes it. Notice what you see, smell, and hear. You can do this either by yourself or in a group—with one person reading while the others go through this imaginative exercise. When you are done, take a moment to write down (or share with one another) what you experienced, who you were in the story, and how you felt as that person as the story unfolded.

SMALL GROUP QUESTIONS ─────────────────────────────

1. What do you think of when you hear the word "justice"? How would you describe God's justice? Can you give an example?

2. What do you think of when you hear the word "mercy"? How would you describe the mercy of God? Can you give an example?

3. "This is why the Father loves me, because I lay down my life in order to take it up again. No one takes it from me, but I lay it down on my own. I have power to lay it down, and power to take it up again" (John 10:17-18). Why do you think it was important that Jesus laid down his life of his own accord?

4. What are the characteristics of the new and final covenant that God has made with his people? How was that covenant sealed, and why is that so important?

5. How does knowing more about what Jesus suffered on the cross influence or change your understanding of the

Crucifixion? Do you see any connection between the crucifixion of Jesus and your own life? What difference does Jesus' death on the cross make in your life right now?

6. How would you describe to others why Jesus laid down his life on the cross?

7. If you have reflected on the Scripture passages in the Further Reflection section, what parts of the Passion Narrative struck you or moved you when you read them?

CHAPTER 5

The Kingdom Cannot Be Contained—Resurrection

After Jesus' death, the disciples hide away in fear.

Think about it. Their teacher, their friend, the Messiah in whom they have placed their hopes for the liberation of the Jewish people, the one who healed the sick and raised the dead, now lies dead himself, his body battered by the Roman soldiers and the merciless weight of the cross. The crowds that once followed Jesus, hanging on his every word, have turned against him, demanding that he be crucified. As his closest friends, the disciples fear for their very lives. So, they hide behind locked doors "for fear of the Jews" (John 20:19).

In their fear, fueled by grief and shock, they must be questioning everything—their own decision to follow Jesus, their every experience while with him, and all of the things that he did and said. Where now is the power of the one who walked on water? Where is the brilliant teacher who could confound the most learned of the Pharisees with his wisdom? What of the Father's love and the promised restoration of Israel? Was it all just a lie, a kindhearted ruse that finally went too far? What of this man, Jesus, whom they all believed to be holy? Now his very death seems to show him to be accursed (for the Jews believed that anyone hung upon a pole and killed was cursed, according to Deuteronomy 21:22–23). If he wasn't sent from God, then who have they been following?

In the three days following Jesus' crucifixion, his beloved disciples hear only silence in response to their agonized questions. Yet the Father never just leaves his children to suffer in the midst of tragedy and death. What good father ever would?

Despite the silence, something profound is occurring. Remember, this story is not simply an earthly one. Rather, it is a cosmic story that encompasses all facets of creation. There is an ancient sermon, written by an unknown author, that gives a clear and moving account of the profound breadth and depth of the Father's loving activity during this time:

> What is happening? Today there is a great silence over the earth, a great silence, and stillness, a great silence because the King sleeps; the earth was in terror and was still, because God slept in the flesh and raised up those who were sleeping from the ages. God has died in the flesh, and the underworld has trembled.

> Truly he goes to seek out our first parent like a lost sheep; he wishes to visit those who sit in darkness and in the shadow of death. He goes to free the prisoner Adam and his fellow prisoner, Eve, from their pains, he who is God, and Adam's son.

> The Lord goes to them holding his victorious weapon, his cross. When Adam, the first created man, sees

him, he strikes his breast in terror and calls out to all: "My Lord be with you all." And Christ in reply says to Adam: "And with your spirit." And grasping his hand he raises him up, saying: "Awake, O sleeper, and arise from the dead, and Christ shall give you light."[9]

Although the disciples are not aware of this yet in their grief and hopelessness, a stunning reality is already unfolding. The grave cannot bind the Son of God; it holds no power over him. Even while his body lies dead, Jesus, as prophet of the kingdom of God, continues to reach out to those in most need of mercy and grace—namely, all those men and women who had ever been created, from Adam and Eve's fall up to the death of Jesus. Jesus literally descends into the place reserved for those who lived upright lives, but who died before Jesus' saving death. That's why we recite the words, "He descended into hell" in the Apostles' Creed. Beginning with our first parents, Jesus invites them all to life, and at last opens up the gates of the kingdom to them.

Simply put, the kingdom of God cannot be contained, not even by death. It is the manifestation of the Father's love. Jesus, the one who truly restores, bears the good news of salvation to those who first rejected the kingdom, and to all their heirs who have died. And the story doesn't end there. Christ does not accomplish his saving work only for those who had already lived and died. Three days after his death, he rises in glory for all those who still live and all who will yet

---

[9] "The Lord's descent into hell," from an ancient homily for Holy Saturday, Pontifical University of Saint Thomas Aquinas, http://www.vatican.va/spirit/documents/spirit_20010414_omelia-sabato-santo_en.html.

live. Breaking the chains of death, the most powerful of the Enemy's works, the Father raises Jesus to new life.

For the disciples, still reeling from the horror of their teacher's torture and death, the reality of the resurrection of Jesus Christ breaks into their grief as a startled proclamation from several women, among them Mary Magdalene, Joanna, and Mary, the mother of James. According to Luke 24, these women come with spices to the tomb of Jesus, wanting to attend to his body. There, they find the tomb empty, and "two men in dazzling garments" (angels) appear to them, asking, "Why do you seek the living among the dead?" (Luke 24:4–5). These angels tell them clearly that Jesus has been raised from the dead, and the women immediately go to the eleven disciples. Becoming in a very real sense the apostles to the apostles, these women pass on what they have seen and heard.

The news spreads like wildfire. Peter and John run to the tomb to discover for themselves that Jesus' body is no longer there. If this were simply the case of a missing body, perhaps this would be the end of the story. As we soon see, however, this is not a case of a stolen corpse. In fact, the risen Jesus begins to appear to his disciples:

- In the Gospel of John, a distraught Mary Magdalene is worrying about where they have taken the body of her Lord, only to discover that Jesus himself is speaking to her right outside the tomb (see 20:11–18).

- On the road to Emmaus, two disciples encounter a stranger as they talk about the terrible things that happened to Jesus in Jerusalem. This stranger teaches them about the prophecies in the Hebrew Scriptures that point to Jesus. They break bread with the stranger, and in the breaking of the bread, he reveals himself to them as Jesus (Luke 24:13–35).

- He appears to the disciples in Jerusalem, convincing them he is not a ghost by taking food with them (Luke 24:36–49).

- Jesus reveals himself to the disciples again at the Sea of Tiberius, eventually eating breakfast with them and having a personal exchange with Peter, in which he forgives Peter for denying him three times during his trial and torture (John 21:1–19).

- He appears to his disciples right before his ascension and urges them to make disciples of all nations, baptizing in the name of the Father, the Son, and the Holy Spirit, and passing on to the world what he taught to them (Matthew 28:16–20).

The appearances of Jesus to his disciples don't stop there. The apostle Paul records in his First Letter to the Corinthians that Jesus appeared "to more than five hundred brothers at once" (15:6). Luke, the author of a Gospel and the Acts of the Apostles, also records, "He presented himself alive to them by many proofs after he had suffered, appearing to them during forty days and speaking about the kingdom of God" (Acts 1:3).

Why emphasize these facts? If the coming of Jesus Christ represents the fulfillment of the Great Story of salvation, then

his resurrection from the dead is the climax of that fulfillment—the definitive moment of the Father's love renewing
all of creation through his Son.

In the Old Testament story of Noah, God sends a flood
to destroy his rebellious creatures, sparing only Noah and his
family, along with a pair of every kind of animal (see Genesis
6:5–7). In the resurrection of Jesus Christ, the earth is now
flooded with the divine life of God, breaking apart what St.
Paul calls "the elemental powers of the world" and bringing
with it the possibility of new life, restoration, and wholeness
(Colossians 2:20). In the Genesis account, only Noah and his
family are spared; in the resurrection of Jesus, the whole created order is suffused with the resurrected power of Christ,
and there is at last a possibility for the whole human race to
live fully in the kingdom of God.

Pope Francis highlights this reality in a passage from his
apostolic exhortation *The Joy of the Gospel*:

> Christ's resurrection is not an event of the past; it con-
> tains a vital power which has permeated this world.
> Where all seems to be dead, signs of the resurrec-
> tion suddenly spring up. It is an irresistible force....
> Christ's resurrection everywhere calls forth seeds of
> that new world; even if they are cut back, they grow
> again, for the resurrection is already secretly woven
> into the fabric of this history, for Jesus did not rise
> in vain.[10]

The greatest military and political power in the ancient
world focused its might on the Son of God. The enemies

---

[10] Pope Francis, *Evangelii Gaudium* ("The Joy of the Gospel"), 276–8.

of God's kingdom arrayed themselves against Christ, God's anointed one. The elemental powers of the world and all the works of the devil came crashing down on Jesus, who offered himself freely as a sign of the Father's love. He was beaten, insulted, and ultimately killed. If the story ended here, hopelessness would rule us. There would be no escape from the dictatorship of death and the mastery of sin. Indeed, as Paul wrote:

> But if Christ is preached as raised from the dead, how can some among you say there is no resurrection of the dead? If there is no resurrection of the dead, then neither has Christ been raised. And if Christ has not been raised, then empty [too] is our preaching; empty, too, your faith. Then we are also false witnesses to God, because we testified against God that he raised Christ, whom he did not raise if in fact the dead are not raised. For if the dead are not raised, neither has Christ been raised, and if Christ has not been raised, your faith is vain; you are still in your sins. Then those
>
> who have fallen asleep in Christ have perished. If for this life only we have hoped in Christ, we are the most pitiable people of all. (1 Corinthians 15:12–19)

The good news about the Good News is that Jesus is truly risen. The Resurrection is a historical event witnessed by a great many people—witnesses who had nothing to gain and everything to lose by proclaiming belief in someone who was put to death by Jewish religious leaders and the powerful Roman Empire. The accounts of the appearances of Jesus to his disciples underscore the reality of the Resurrection. Jesus has not been simply "spiritually resurrected," as some argue, or kept alive in the memory of his followers. Rather, the Son of God was truly killed and truly raised bodily from the dead. The *whole* Jesus has risen to new life. His disciples are able to touch his physical wounds (see John 20:24–29), and Jesus frequently eats and drinks with them. Though his body is glorified, no longer limited by the laws of this world (for instance, the Gospel writers record Jesus entering locked rooms), Jesus is not a ghost but a real man.

The power of God has triumphed over all the enemies of his kingdom. Jesus' resurrection means that he truly is the Messiah, the Son of God. The Resurrection validates everything that Jesus claimed about his identity. That means his teachings also are all valid, especially those teachings that reveal who we are as beloved sons and daughters of God. Furthermore, if he is the Son of God and his teachings are true, then we also can hold on to hope for eternal life and a place in the kingdom of our Father.

Jesus' resurrection shifts and changes everything! The Son of God has died for us, and death cannot hold him. That means we are no longer subject to the powers of sin and death. This is why Paul would write so powerfully: "Death is swallowed up in victory. / Where, O death, is your victory? / Where, O death, is your sting?" (1 Corinthians 15:54–55). We hear this celebration of victory in an ancient hymn from the Eastern Churches, *Christos Anesti* ("Christ Is Risen"):

Christ is risen from the dead,
by death trampling down upon death,
and to those in the tombs he has granted life.

UP, UP, BUT NOT AWAY

Luke records in his Gospel: "Then he led them [out] as far as Bethany, raised his hands, and blessed them. As he blessed them he parted from them and was taken up to heaven" (24:50–51). Jesus' triumph does not simply extend to the Resurrection, but also to his ascension. After appearing to his disciples and imparting on them the mission to make disciples of all nations, Jesus takes his leave of his disciples and returns to the Father.

Growing up, I never understood why we made such a big deal about Jesus' ascension. After all, I reasoned, Jesus was just returning to where he belonged. It wasn't until much later, when I was in my thirties and studying theology seriously, that I began to understand just how powerful Jesus' ascension was. Because Jesus lived through our human nature, that nature ascended with him. Thus our human nature now sits at the right hand of the Father and lives in the very center of the love between the Father, Son, and Holy Spirit. In Jesus, the Father has done more than restore what Adam and Eve's disobedience lost—he has made our nature even better. Since our human nature has been taken up into the Trinity, we now have the possibility of an even deeper communion with God than Adam and Eve had. This is why the Church prays in the ancient *Exsultet* at the Easter Vigil: "O happy fault! O necessary sin of Adam that gained for us so great a redeemer."

The God who is love takes the most tragic act in history—the Crucifixion, as the result of Adam and Eve's sin—and, in the faithfulness of his Son, transforms it into an instrument of surpassing power and joy. On a cosmic level, the Father, who has raised Jesus from the dead, now exalts him in the Ascension, seating him in the place of honor at his right hand. This is a fulfillment of the prophecy found in Psalm 110:1: "The LORD says to my lord: / 'Sit at my right hand / while I make your footstool.'" More than that, it is also closely related to the establishment of Christ as king over all of creation. At the Ascension, the Father places Jesus in the seat of honor and makes him the ruler of his kingdom, which has broken forth into the created order.

Yet we just need to look around to realize that the world is still not perfect. How can we claim that the kingdom is real in any way while so much brokenness, evil, violence, and sickness still exist? The reality is that the Bible speaks of a time when God will create "new heavens and a new earth; / The former things shall not be remembered / nor come to mind" (Isaiah 65:17). Jesus himself promised many times that the Son of Man would come again, a kind of final work of the kingdom. Jesus' resurrection inaugurates God's kingdom, but it has not yet been made manifest in all its fullness. Therefore, we live in the time between the coming of God's kingdom and its full and total manifestation among us. In this time of tension between the *already* and the *not yet*, the healing and restorative power of the kingdom is at work, even in the face of great opposition.

Pope Francis highlights what life is like in this intervening time before God's kingdom will reign in fullness among us:

All around us we see persistent injustice, evil, indifference and cruelty. But it is also true that in the midst of darkness something new always springs to life and sooner or later produces fruit. On razed land life breaks through, stubbornly yet invincibly. However dark things are, goodness always re-emerges and spreads. Each day in our world beauty is born anew, it rises transformed through the storms of history. Values always tend to reappear under new guises, and human beings have arisen time after time from situations that seemed doomed. Such is the power of the resurrection.[11]

Perhaps an analogy might help make this real. It's an old one, but a good one. On June 6, 1944, American, British, and Canadian forces landed on the beaches of Normandy to launch an amphibious invasion to liberate France and defeat the Germans during World War II. The Allies' victory in Normandy essentially broke the power of the Germans. The war was, in essence, over—though fighting continued until the Germans surrendered officially on May 8, 1945. That day is celebrated as V-E Day, or Victory in Europe Day. In this analogy, the resurrection of Jesus is D-Day, that definitive moment when the kingdom of God in Jesus Christ shattered the powers of the Enemy. We live now in the time between D-Day and V-E Day. The forces of the Enemy are still at work, still resisting, still trying to slow and block the advancement of the kingdom of God. However, the war is already won, and Satan is, ultimately, fighting a retreat.

WHAT'S IN IT FOR ME?

At this point, you might be wondering what all of this has to do with you. We have been dealing with the cosmic realities

---

[11] Ibid., 276.

of the Resurrection, but perhaps the most powerful implications of the Resurrection pertain to you. The purpose of the life, death, resurrection, and ascension of Jesus wasn't simply to liberate humanity in the abstract. For God, the multiple billions of people who live, and who have ever lived, on the earth are not nameless, faceless creatures. They are beloved sons and daughters. The reality is that the Father raised Jesus from the dead so that you and I could experience freedom and new life.

The Father restored Jesus to life, filling him with the power of the Resurrection, the power of the kingdom of God. Although Jesus was a divine person with a divine nature, he chose to take on our human nature and live among us. He is truly one of us. Because Jesus bears our nature, because God made common cause with us and became human, we now have access to the divine and resurrected life of Jesus Christ. As God, Jesus invites us into communion with him through baptism so that the divine life might penetrate our human nature, freeing us and transforming us to become like him. Paul proclaims this in a clear way when he writes: "We were indeed buried with him through baptism into death, so that, just as Christ was raised from the dead by the glory of the Father, we too might live in newness of life" (Romans 6:4).

Christ does not hoard the gift of resurrected life like a treasure hidden away in some locked vault. Rather, just as he gave his life away on the cross, so he freely offers the resurrected life of the kingdom to all who desire it. Indeed, his great desire is that all would experience new life. In the subtle and wide workings of his grace, he plants that desire in the human heart, patiently tilling the soil until desire for his kingdom can sprout there. He nurtures that desire with his body and blood, and he rejoices as it grows stronger until the heart cries out for the Father's love.

In his Letter to the Colossians, Paul declares that God "delivered us from the power of darkness and transferred us to the kingdom of his beloved Son" (1:13). In the kingdom of darkness, sin keeps us separated from the Father's love, and death is the final chapter to our story. Under the power of darkness, we are weighed down by our own brokenness and bound in the chains of our fears, limitations, and disordered desires. In the kingdom of God, the Father's love triumphs over the power of sin, and death is no longer the final chapter of our story. In this kingdom the love of God in Jesus lifts the weight and breaks every chain that binds us. For our part, we must continually say "yes" to his invitation to experience more resurrected life.

At Jesus' crucifixion, he saved us *from* the guilt of sin *for* the experience of kingdom life, here and now. We who live in the tension between the appearance of his kingdom and its complete manifestation at the end of time are supposed to experience the realities and fruits of his kingdom as we live in the midst of this world. We are supposed to experience freedom and integrity, healing and wholeness, peace and joy in our lives right now, and not simply in the next life. Living in the kingdom is supposed to be an experience of ever deepening freedom. It is a reconstruction of our identity as sons and daughters. The brokenness of the world may have shaped us, but in the power of the Resurrection, the Lord re-fathers us, returning us to the shape he intended when he created us. Because of the resurrection of Jesus, there is a way through the difficulties of this life. Whatever you are struggling with, whatever pain or brokenness, even the things you suffer silently in the depths of the night when no one is around—there is a way through, a path to transformation and true freedom.

And this way isn't a system of belief, or a set of moral principles. It isn't a regimen of self-help platitudes or mental exercises. The way is simply a person, Jesus Christ … and this Jesus is inviting you right now, as you read this chapter and wrestle with these words. He is inviting you to more—a deeper experience of the love of God. He longs for you to live in the reality of God's kingdom, which, if you are baptized, you have already received.

How do we experience this resurrected life? How can we truly live in the power and the presence of the kingdom of God here and now?

The story continues …

FURTHER REFLECTION

Take some time (at least fifteen minutes a day) and prayerfully read through the following accounts of Jesus' resurrection and his appearances to his disciples:

- Luke 24:1–12

- John 20:1–10

- Luke 24:13–35

- John 20:11–18

- Luke 24:36–49

After you have read through them a few times, read them again, and this time try and imagine yourself in that reading. In other words, picture yourself in the scene as the author describes it. Notice what you see, smell, and hear. You can do this either by yourself or in a group—with one person reading while the others go through this imaginative exercise. When you are done, take a moment to write down (or share with each other) what you experienced, who you were in the story, and how you felt as that person as the story unfolded.

SMALL GROUP QUESTIONS

1. In your own life, can you remember a time when God seemed to be silent and far away—like Jesus in the tomb for three days? Looking back, what are some ways you now see that God was still at work in your life during that dark time?

2. How might the incredible power of Jesus' resurrection transform the way we perceive and deal with suffering and sorrow in our own lives and in the world around us?

3. What does it mean for you that Jesus rose from the dead? Where do you most need the resurrected power of Christ in your own life? Where have you seen the power of the Resurrection in your own life?

4. Why do you think St. Paul tells the Christian community in Corinth that their "faith is vain" if Jesus did not really

rise from the dead? What would you say to people in our own day who dismiss the Resurrection as a myth?

5. As baptized Christians, we now share in the glory of Christ's resurrection—but as long as we are in this world, we have to live in the "not yet" of kingdom life, which means we still struggle with sin. How does the Lord call us to live in this reality? Should we just give up the struggle against sin, or is there a deeper invitation here?

CHAPTER 6

Jesus Invites Us into a Relationship

God has sent you an invitation.

It's an invitation to something real, something tangible. More than a sugary promise of a better life in some distant future, or a vague splash of hope that at some point things will work out, this invitation is to a radical, ongoing encounter with Love that begins right now. This ongoing encounter will reveal who you really are. It will set you on a course driven by purpose and fulfillment, and restore a destiny that was yours before the world began. This invitation is a declaration that the kingdom of God is for you to live in the *here and now*. The characteristics of kingdom life—peace, joy, wholeness, generation, multiplication, a desire to pour oneself out for others—will take hold of you and manifest in and through you as you grow in relationship with the God who created you for himself.

The desire for relationship (knowing and being known, loving and being loved) has been hardwired into us. Why? Because, as we explored earlier in the story, all of us have been made in the image and likeness of God, and God is relationship—an eternal one at that. The Father is forever relating to and loving the Son. The Son is forever relating to and loving the Father. The love between the Father and the Son, their dynamic self-giving, which is the Holy Spirit, is forever relating to each of them. It should come as no surprise, then, that Jesus invites us into relationship. This desire we all have for connection and love is not a flaw, but rather the means to our ultimate fulfillment. Remember, the Great Story began in communion. Adam and Eve lived in perfect relationship with God, each other, and the whole of creation—stemming from the divine life which they received from God. The fall ruptured that perfect relationship, depriving all of us of divine life. In God's goodness, the Father sent the Son to call the whole human race back to himself. Through his life, death, resurrection, and ascension, Jesus has satisfied the Father's justice and mercy, paying the price for sin and making the divine life—the life of the kingdom—once more present and available to all who desire it. Now Jesus invites each of us to receive a share in his very own life, lived in communion with God and one another.

The cosmic scope of the whole story ultimately connects to our own response. Jesus asks us the same question that he asked his disciples: "Who do you say that I am?" (Matthew 16:15). The answer we give to this question determines what we will do with his offer of friendship.

HE'S BACK—AND THIS TIME,
IT'S PERSONAL

One of the most foundational aspects of a relationship with God is that it is personal.

A "personal relationship with God" might be an unfamiliar or uncomfortable concept to a lot of Catholics. Many of us have experienced some of our Christian brothers and sisters asking us if "we have accepted Jesus Christ as our personal Lord and Savior." This notion can feel foreign to our own experience as Catholics. Yet if we examine both Scripture and Tradition closely, we can see that there is nothing more fundamentally Catholic than to speak of a personal relationship with God. We might mean something a little different than our Christian brothers and sisters when we speak of personal relationship, but this kind of relationship is at the heart of the Great Story. In the Gospel of John, Jesus promises, "Whoever loves me will keep my word, and my Father will love him, and we will come to him and make our dwelling with him" (John 14:23). The deepest expression of this promise occurs during the celebration of the Mass, where Catholics receive the gift of Jesus' body and blood, soul and divinity, consuming the whole Lord and taking him into their own body and soul. It's hard to get more personal than that!

This relationship with God is by nature personal, first, because God is personal. (More precisely, he is Personhood itself—but we will leave that concept for the philosophers to figure out.) Looking at Scripture and Tradition, though, we discover that God is actually three Persons, Father, Son, and Holy Spirit, united in one Being and engaged in eternal relationship. To be in relationship with God is to be in relationship with Persons. Pope Benedict, speaking specifically about relationship with Christ, had this to say about the heart of Catholicism: "Being Christian is not the result of an ethical choice or a lofty idea, but the encounter with an event, a person, which gives life a new horizon and a decisive direction."[12] Jesus invites us into a relationship not only with himself, but with the whole Trinity. And this relationship transforms our lives—if we let it.

Like God, we also are persons; each of us has an intellect, a will, and emotions. Whenever one person encounters another person, there is, by definition, an (inter)personal relationship. Such an encounter with another person demands some kind of response from us that emerges out of our personhood. We either engage with that person or keep them at a distance, for a variety of very personal reasons. Therefore, it is fair to say that we make personal choices to enter relationships with other people, and these relationships change us. When we open ourselves up to another person, when we allow ourselves to discover another person, to get to know them and to love them, it does something to us; it shapes our worldview and our understanding of who we are. In the most life-giving of these relationships, we learn to appreciate deeply, and even come to love, the things that our beloved cares deeply about.

I remember when I first started to date the woman who would become my wife. When Debbie and I first met—online of all places—she lived in Chicago and I lived in Seattle. I would fly out every few weeks to spend time with her, but our time together was limited. Imagine my surprise when, during one of our precious afternoons together, she suggested that we watch a few episodes of the original *The Muppet Show*. Now, I'll let you in on a little secret that I never told her while we were dating: I really hated the Muppets! In fact, I couldn't think of any other activity I wanted to do

---

[12] Pope Benedict XVI, *Deus Caritas Est* ("God Is Love"), 1.

less than watch *The Muppet Show.* What a waste of our time together, I thought to myself. However (and I don't know if I mentioned this earlier), my wife is one of the most beautiful and amazing women whom I have ever met. I may not have liked the Muppets, but I was no fool. Here was an incredible woman who wanted to spend time with me. So, I sucked it up and watched endless hours of the Muppets.

Here's the crazy thing, though. Over time, I found myself connecting that time with the Muppets with positive things about my wife. I also watched the delight they brought her, and over time I began to appreciate *The Muppet Show* because it made my wife happy. Our first Christmas together, I found myself scouring the internet to find a complete collection of Muppet finger puppets that one fast-food restaurant was offering with their kids' meals. I wanted to give these to Debbie, inside a vintage Muppet lunchbox, as a gift. I was so excited when I found them all, and soon realized that every time I looked at Muppets, I thought of my wife. Since it was clear to me that I loved her, I almost couldn't help but fall in love with the Muppets. Soon, I found myself suggesting that we watch *The Muppet Show* together!

This may be a silly example, but it illustrates a powerful dimension of a personal relationship with God. We can connect with God in a very intimate and real way because Jesus became one of us. He was a historical figure; he lived in time, among us in this world; he shares our very nature. Yet he is also God. Just as our hearts can change when we enter into a relationship with another human person, how much more will we change when we enter into a relationship with our Creator. The One Who Is Love has radically revealed himself to us in Jesus Christ, and in doing so he has ultimately

revealed who we are in him. He has given us his very life so
that we might fully become the people he created us to be.

Why are we spending so much time on this personal
dimension of a relationship with God? The reality is that
many people, often through no fault of their own, have an
entirely *institutional* relationship with Christ rather than an
intentional or personal one. What does that mean? It means
that many people participate in the external practices of their
faith—they pray specific prayers, participate in devotions
like the Rosary, attend Mass, go to religious education or
adult faith formation classes—without forming any explicit
personal connection with Jesus. The power and presence of
God's kingdom, the breaking forth of the love of God in the
everyday realities of life, is largely invisible to them. There is
a kind of transactional mentality to this purely institutional
relationship. The sense is that if I "do this thing" and "fulfill
that obligation," I will be rewarded in some specific way, often involving getting to heaven (whatever that might actually
mean to the person in particular). What Jesus actually has to
do with it is somewhat nebulous. This kind of transactional
relationship does not bring peace, but often fear and a sense
of condemnation.

Of course, embracing obligation and the discipline of
following what the Church asks us to do are instrumental in
building and shaping a deep intimacy with God. Yet there is
far more to being in this relationship with God than "following rules." The Lord desires not just external fidelity to ritual,
but also internal conversion, the participation of the heart,
which is the center of the whole person. That's why the Lord
would remind the Israelites in the Old Testament that when
confronted by their own brokenness and sinfulness, the best

response was to "rend your heart, not your garments" (Joel 2:13).

St. Paul goes even further. In his Letter to the Ephesians, he uses marital language to express the kind of engagement of the heart that God desires with his people. The Church is his bride; he is the Bridegroom. That kind of personal, deeply intimate relationship is the model for us. As I have heard it said, far too many people experience the Church not as the Bride of Christ, but as the widow of Christ—as if Christ were dead and gone, and far removed from the everyday life of his bride.

Nothing could be further from the truth. The Great Story of Jesus is a clarion call, a declaration of love made over all of God's people, and an invitation to enter the depths of that love.

AN UNDESERVED INVITATION

This invitation to a relationship with God is completely undeserved. It is critically important that we really understand this truth. The freedom we have in Christ over the power of sin, the ultimate victory over death, the restoration of communion with the Father—none of it results from our own merit. It is all a free gift from God through his Son, Jesus. The stain of Original Sin, and the complications of our own personal choices to disobey God, place us out of communion with him. Apart from the saving power and life of Jesus Christ, no amount of good deeds, hours spent in prayer, decades of the Rosary, or time spent in church can change that.

The reality is that the Father didn't send his Son into the world to save us because of who *we* are. Rather, he paid the price for our salvation and now offers us new life because of who *he* is. He is perfect Fatherhood, and he calls us back as his sons and daughters. Think about that! Though many people have not experienced loving and authentic parenting in their lives, the truth is that children should never have to earn the love of their parents. That love flows out of a parent's identity, and it is expressed in the context of a relationship. In the perfect Fatherhood of God, there is not a single thing that you or I can do to change the way God thinks about or loves us. His love flows from who he is. This means that there is nothing, not a single activity (including studying harder, losing weight, being kinder to others, going to church more, etc.) that will make God love us any more than he does right now.

In other words, God doesn't love us because we are good. Rather, we are good because God loves us. We can't earn his love—it's freely given.

There is something tremendously freeing in that truth. So many of us get caught up in a kind of "performance" Christianity, sure that God won't really love us until we "get better." Without realizing it, we are driven by this sense of unworthiness and the lie that "if only" we were different then God would love us. We see our imperfections as disqualifying us from receiving the transforming love of Jesus Christ. We think we must stumble through this life as best we can, hoping that God will let us squeak by into purgatory—at best. At worst, too many of us fatalistically determine that we will never be with God in heaven.

The power and light of the Great Story breaks apart that lie and all the darkness surrounding it. Another way of stating the Gospel message could be this: **You can't fix yourself; only God can do that, but he's waiting for you to let him.** True transformation and lasting healing only come from an experience of God's love. And the truth is that God is crazy in love with you *right now*, for who you are *right now*, with all your faults and foibles. Your brokenness, the history of your failures, and even what has been done to you through the brokenness of others, cannot triumph over the love of God in Jesus Christ—that same love that is offered freely to all, and especially to you in this moment as you read this chapter.

Don't think that's possible? God has made it clear that nothing is impossible for him. Remember, Jesus came back from the dead, breaking the power of Satan ... for us.

NOT "ME" BUT "WE"

This relationship offered to us by God is intimate and personal, but it is not solitary.

The Lord saves us as a people and invites us into communion not just with him, but with one another. Kingdom life is a life lived in communion with God and his people. As baptized Christians, we follow Christ as real members of his mystical body, which is the Church. This idea of the Church as a body comes from St. Paul, in his Letter to the Corinthians. This is more than an empty metaphor; it is the expression of a deep connectedness that all the baptized share. We are so linked to one another through Jesus, who is the head of the body, that Paul writes: "If [one] part suffers, all the parts suffer with it; if one part is honored, all the parts share its joy" (1 Corinthians 12:26).

Indeed, so powerful is the reality of the Church as a body that, according to Paul, this has become our primary identity: "Now you are Christ's body, and individually parts of it" (1 Corinthians 12:27). Even before we are individuals, the baptized are part of the covenant people of God, set in communion with him in such intimacy that we are one body.

The profound relationship of our first parents with each other is now expressed in the New Covenant of Jesus Christ. Why is that so important? First, it means that there is a deeper connection between all of God's people—the entire human race—than we could hope to realize. This connection is taken to its deepest level for those baptized into the life and body of Christ. In a very literal sense, it means that our lives don't make sense apart from one another. The communal dimension of relationship with Christ is a pledge and declaration from Jesus that we need never be alone and isolated again; we will always have a place, a purpose, and a home. Living with and for each other in Christ also means that no one's life is superfluous, able to be cast away without notice or comment—including yours.

WHO, ME?

As the Great Story unfolds now, your choices matter. Jesus' invitation to experience the power of his love and to live filled with kingdom life is not a generic one. Just as the Father called out specifically to Adam and asked, "Where are you?" so now the Father is calling out to you. He is speaking over you his Word, Jesus Christ, and this Jesus sees into the depths of your heart as he invites you: "Come to me, all you who labor and are burdened, and I will give you rest. Take my yoke upon you and learn from me, for I am meek and humble of heart; and you will find rest for yourselves. For my yoke is easy, and my burden light" (Matthew 11:28–30).

The One who created you is calling you by name. "Behold," he says, "I stand at the door, and knock" (Revelation 3:20). Without prejudice, without judgment, the One who knows everything about you, who sees into the secret places, stands at the door of your heart and offers mercy and new life today. What would it take to say "yes" to that invitation? What holds you back? The weight of the guilt you feel, the unworthiness or shame that binds you, is not too heavy for the One who carried the wood of the cross on his shoulders. The pain and the loneliness you may have felt throughout your life are not beyond the understanding and power of the One who died on Calvary abandoned by nearly everyone he loved. The hopelessness and frustration at the circumstances of life, the damage you may have done to yourself and to others, cannot overwhelm the forgiveness of Jesus, who destroyed the works of Satan when he burst forth from the tomb. Nothing is beyond the Father's love in Jesus Christ, and he offers that love to you now.

Jesus awaits you. Will you meet him?

FURTHER REFLECTION

Take some time (at least fifteen minutes a day) and prayerfully read through the following accounts of Jesus calling his disciples:

- Matthew 4:18–22

- Mark 1:16–34

- Luke 5:1–11

After you have read through these passages a few times, read them again, and this time try to imagine yourself in that reading. In other words, picture yourself in the scene as the author describes it. Notice what you see, smell, and hear. You can do this either by yourself or in a group with one person reading while the others go through this imaginative exercise. When you are done, take a moment to write down (or share with each other) what you experienced, who you were in the story, and how you felt as that person as the story unfolded.

SMALL GROUP QUESTIONS

1. What one word immediately comes to mind when you reflect on your current relationship with God? Whatever word popped into your head first, hold onto that and ponder it for a few minutes. Are you happy with it? How might God be calling you to let him in just a little bit more?

2. Have you ever been asked if you have accepted Jesus Christ as your personal Lord and Savior? If yes, how do you respond to that question? After reading this book so far, has your response changed in any way?

3. In your own words describe what it means to have a personal relationship with Jesus.

4. As baptized Christians, we truly are members of Jesus' mystical body, which means each of us has a unique and specific role to play in God's kingdom. Have you ever prayed to know more deeply what your special role is—what "part" of the body you are? If yes, how did God make the answer known to you? If no, consider asking him now what unique role he has for you in his body, the Church.

5. Has there been a time in your life when you felt particularly called by God to do something (perhaps a one-time event like a retreat or a call to change your life in a radical way)? How did you respond to the call? What happened next?

6. What would it take to say "yes" to a deeper relationship with Jesus? What holds you back?

CHAPTER 7

Jesus Asks for Our Repentance

G od will not be content with having just part of you. He wants all of you. Not just the good parts, or the faithful parts, or the parts of your life where you're fairly confident that you "have it together"—he wants it all, especially the messy parts of your life. Maybe that comes as a surprise. So often we hold to an image of God as a "spiritual germophobe" or a kind of disapproving, aristocratic fussbucket who sniffs with disdain at the merest mention or sign of imperfection.

THE JUNK ROOM

My wife, Debbie, my daughter, Siena, and I live in a 1,000-square-foot townhome with two Siberian huskies. To say that it can get a little cramped is a bit of an understatement. In a place that small, it is quite easy for things to get cluttered. My travel schedule, coupled with Debbie's work schedule and our daughter's extracurricular activities, often results in our house looking like a tornado has swept through it. Debbie loves to entertain, however—which means that the day before we have any guests over we are frantically cleaning. In a house the size of ours, it is rare that we can find a place for everything. Therefore, at some point during our cleaning frenzy we start tossing all of the misfit items—the junk—into my daughter's room upstairs, and we shut the door.

Downstairs the next day, our guests might have an amazing experience—scented candles cast soft light, the sound of music fills the space, and the smell of great food permeates everywhere. My wife and I come across as great hosts who have it together. Upstairs, though, my daughter's door is swelling from the pressure of all the junk that we've crammed into her room.

That's how many people feel they must approach the Lord, shoving all of the junk in their lives into another room, or sweeping it under the table and putting a nice tablecloth over it before daring to speak to him. Even worse, some people don't believe he will listen at all because they have that junk in their lives, so they don't even try to speak with him. Yet the testimony of the Bible—God's word—reveals quite a different picture. Far from simply being angry or condemning us because of our brokenness, God chooses willingly to become one of us. The One who is Perfection has taken on our human nature and lived as one of us. Even during his earthly life, the Son of God chose to spend time not just with the righteous and holy but with those who were cast off from society—prostitutes, thieves, tax collectors, drunks, and other shady characters. When confronted about this by the religious leaders of his day, Jesus replied: "Those who are healthy do not need a physician, but the sick do. I have not come to call the righteous to repentance but sinners" (Luke 5:31–32).

God will not be content with having just part of you. That truth was clear from the moment the Lord made his covenant with the Israelites through Moses, giving them the Ten Commandments. In the very First Commandment, the Lord says:

I am the LORD your God, who brought you out of the land of Egypt, out of the house of slavery. You shall not have other gods beside me. You shall not make for yourself an idol or a likeness of anything in the heavens above or on the earth below or in the waters beneath the earth; you shall not bow down before them or serve them. For I, the LORD, your God, am a jealous God. (Exodus 20:2–5)

The jealousy of God is not an imperfection like ours is. It does not flow out of vanity or pettiness on his part. Rather, the Father knows that since we are created for relationship with him, the fulfillment of our lives rests in him alone. He is jealous of our love, our time, our attention, not because he needs it, but because he knows that we do. The more our hearts are divided the more distracted we are from receiving and living fully the kingdom life that Jesus invites us to.

We can see this in the story of the rich young man who comes to Jesus and asks him what he must do to gain eternal life (see Mark 10:17–22). Jesus tells the young man to live faithfully the covenant God made with Moses by keeping the commandments. The man replies that he has kept the commandments all his life. Then Jesus instructs the young man to sell everything he has, give it to the poor, and then to "come, follow me." In the last line of that encounter, we read of the young man that "his face fell, and he went away sad, for he had many possessions" (10:22). It is important to note here that merely possessing great wealth is not what keeps this young man from the kingdom; in a moral sense wealth is neither good nor bad. What keeps him from living kingdom life is the reality that his wealth has divided his heart. He doesn't so much possess this wealth; it possesses him.

God will not be content with having just part of you. He longs for each of us to have an undivided heart. The Father knows that the contents of our personal "junk room" keep us from giving all of ourselves to him, and so he sent Jesus to free us from that junk. The invitation to a relationship that we explored in the last chapter of the Great Story is precisely this—an invitation to be set free from the junk. We do not need to live with that room anymore; it no longer has to hold any power over our thoughts, relationships, hopes, dreams, or actions.

This process of handing over our junk to Jesus is called repentance. It is the way our relationship with Jesus begins. He himself would declare this necessary step from the earliest moments of his earthly ministry when he said, "Repent, for the kingdom of heaven is at hand" (Matthew 4:17). The way to enter into the kingdom, which is present among us in the person of Jesus, is to unburden ourselves of the things that keep us from God. We offer them to him to dispose of.

When I was a child, I loved visiting my grandparents. My family lived in Long Island, New York, and we would pack into my dad's blue Ford van and drive about two and one half hours to where my *oma* and *opa* (yes, I come from a very German family) lived. Almost immediately upon arriving, I would investigate what candy Oma had in the glass jar in the living room (usually she had M&Ms). My parents limited me to one handful of candies. I thought this was patently unfair, but now that I have a young child of my own, I see that my parents were simply playing good defense!

I remember one time running into the living room and stuffing my hand full of those M&Ms—only to have Oma tell me that she had a surprise for me. I turned around to see my grandmother holding out a bag of the only candy I liked more than plain M&Ms—peanut M&Ms! Now, what you might not know about me is that I have a congenital birth defect. I was born without a hand on my right arm. So, in order for me to get those peanut M&Ms, I was going to have to let go of the regular M&Ms in my hand. It took me many, many years to realize the powerful lesson in that experience: often, we need to let go of the things we think are good for us, or the things we habitually desire, in order to receive something that is even better for us. How can we be filled with the very life of God that Jesus offers us if our hearts are already stuffed with things that are not from God?

The question becomes: What things am I holding on to that I need to give to the Lord?

THE BURDEN OF SIN

Our society doesn't like to talk about sin all that much—it seems too judgmental or old-fashioned. Refusing to talk about something that is real, however, doesn't make that reality disappear. In fact, when we don't talk about certain topics because they make us uncomfortable or we don't want to deal with them, they tend to grow in power and affect us in ways that we can't begin to see.

The Church calls sin "an offense against reason, truth, and right conscience; it is failure in genuine love for God and neighbor caused by a perverse attachment to certain goods. It wounds the nature of man and injures human solidarity. It has been defined as 'an utterance, a deed, or a desire contrary to the eternal law.'"[13] That's a chunky definition, and it uses some pretty stark language. If we look back at the earliest parts of the Great Story, though, the definition begins to make more sense.

Remember, we were created to live in a deep, intimate relationship with God. Simply put, sin consists of any thoughts or actions that disrupt or wound that relationship. Because that relationship is communal (we are in a relationship with all those whom God loves), actions, words, and even thoughts that disrupt or hurt those relationships also wound our relationship with God. When we place our own needs before those of others, when we pay more attention to objects than people, or when we allow created things to draw our attention away from our Creator, we are straying down the path of sin.

St. Paul, speaking of the human condition after the fall, wrote that "all have sinned and are deprived of the glory of God" (Romans 3:23). We may not call it sin, but all of us struggle with making the right choices—and none of us makes the right choice every time. Perhaps the language of "sin and virtue" is unfamiliar to us, but all of us are familiar with the effects of sin in our lives. We make plans with the best of intentions, resolutions to treat others better, to take better care of ourselves, to stop reacting in the destructive

---

[13] *Catechism of the Catholic Church*, 1849.

ways we habitually do when confronted with a certain person or type of situation—and then we fail. Paul recognized this in his own life and wrote with remarkable honesty about it to the Church in Rome: "What I do, I do not understand. For I do not do what I want, but I do what I hate.... For I do not do the good I want, but I do the evil I do not want" (Romans 7:15–19).

Again, the good news is that Jesus has already broken the power of sin and paid the price of our sinfulness. Turning away from the power of sin and turning to God, asking his forgiveness, is the definition of repentance. This idea is embedded in the Greek word for repentance, *metanoia*, which carries with it the reality of a change of mind, or a turning in a new direction. When we allow the Lord Jesus into the junk of our sin, the power of his life brings not only forgiveness but the strength to walk that change out in our lives. That's why the apostle John would write: "If we say, 'We are without sin,' we deceive ourselves, and the truth is not in us. If we acknowledge our sins, he is faithful and just, and will forgive our sins and cleanse us from every wrongdoing" (1 John 1:8–9).

THE BURDEN OF BROKENNESS

Sin is the worst kind of virus. Once we sin, we not only incur the guilt of sin and rupture our relationship with God, but the sinful act itself has a negative effect on us and the world. On us, it wounds our conscience and darkens our intellect, making it more difficult to recognize when a future action would be sinful. It also makes us susceptible to shame, fear, self-accusation, and self-hatred.

When we sin, it also has an effect on the world around us—especially if that sin involved another person. Think about the burdens we carry in our lives because of the sinful actions of others toward us. When we bear the brunt of someone else's anger, accusation, or abuse, it affects us. The world itself also suffers because of the presence of sin. Tragedy and evil are a part of the experience of life in this world. Bad things sometimes do happen to good people. This experience of living in a fallen world makes its mark on us, leaving us feeling weighed down and broken.

Because of our interconnectedness, sin is never a completely solitary experience. It has a social dimension. One thing that we are very sensitive to in our contemporary culture is injustice, particularly the presence of collective, social, or cultural systems of injustice that perpetuate an evil. Sometimes these are called social sins—though that is a misnomer, as only moral agents can commit sin, and a culture itself is not a moral agent. Cultures are, however, made up of individual moral agents, and the overlapping sinful choices we make about a particular area of life can, across the generations, create a systemic injustice that degrades the entire culture. Social injustice, then, is created and fueled by the sinful choices of individuals.

The good news is that Jesus wants to take the burdens of our brokenness along with the guilt of our sinfulness. In the Book of Revelation, when the author saw a new heaven and a new earth, "The one who sat on the throne said, 'I make all things new'" (21:5). Jesus wants us to experience this newness of life in its fullness, and that begins when we give him the burdens of our sin and brokenness. If you are ready to begin that relationship, restore that relationship, or deepen that relationship—if you are ready to acknowledge your thirst and to drink from the One who will satisfy every need, then find a quiet place where you can sit comfortably for a few moments before you begin the next section of this chapter.

It's time for you to take an intentional part in the Great Story of Jesus.

FURTHER REFLECTION

Once you've found a quiet place, take some time to think about all of the things that have been weighing you down, all of the burdens you have been carrying, some maybe from childhood. Reflect on the times when your own actions hurt your relationship with God and with others. The time has come to let the Lord into the junk room, that place in your heart that you keep hidden and secret from all other people.

When you are ready to give the Lord those things which have burdened you, take one hand and rest it, palm up, on your leg. Take your other hand and place it over your heart. Then, take some time and "physically" pull out each of your burdens, your brokenness, the sorrow over your sin—name them quietly and then place each of them in your open hand. Continue doing this until you have nothing left to pull out. During this time, you may feel a surge or rush of emotions, or if you deal with an inner voice that accuses you a great deal, you may hear that voice accusing you loudly. Simply acknowledge those experiences, and continue to pull those burdens out of your heart.

When you are done, place the hand that did the pulling underneath the hand that received all of those burdens. You'll be physically lifting everything you placed in your hand up to the Lord as you pray the following prayer of surrender to the Lord Jesus:

Prayer of Surrender to Jesus

Heavenly Father, I thank you for creating me in your image and likeness. Father, I thank you for making me your beautiful son/daughter.

You know my heart, and my history, and you know that I can't always accept the love that you have for me. Today, I ask for the grace to give you my burdens [You can be specific here: lies, wounds, self-hatred, etc., based on what it is you are praying for.] *and my sorrow for sin, and never to take them up again.*

In the name of Jesus Christ, and by the power of his cross, I break now all power and all authority that these [burdens, lies, wounds, etc.] *have over my life. I declare myself free in the love and power of Jesus Christ.*

Today, I choose to stand in the freedom of the kingdom of God. I know that my identity does not depend on what I have done, or what has been done to me, but rather rests only on your love for me.

I declare that love over my life and receive it with an open heart. And so, Father, I ask that you take these [lies, burdens, wounds, etc.]—

LIFT UP YOUR HANDS AS IF YOU WERE TOSSING THOSE BURDENS YOU PULLED OUT OF YOUR HEART UP TO THE LORD

—and unite them with the wounds of your Son on the

cross. And in exchange, pour forth new life, kingdom life in me! I thank you, Father, for the freedom and healing you are bringing me now. I love you, Lord, and desire to give you my whole heart—even if I have no idea what that might mean at this time in my life.

Lord Jesus, you have called me back to the Father, and I declare that you are the Lord of my life. I acknowledge my sinfulness and humbly come before your throne of mercy. I am yours—a son/daughter of the Most High God. Teach me to love and to become even more fully what you have created me to be.

I ask this in your most precious, most glorious name— Jesus Christ!

If you are Catholic and have received first Reconciliation, then it is important that you make the time, as soon as possible, to receive the Sacrament of Reconciliation. It isn't enough for us to offer our sorrow symbolically to the Lord; we must receive the forgiveness that comes to us through this sacrament, united to Jesus' sacrifice on the cross. Even if you are not yet Catholic, take some time to find someone at the local Catholic parish or a Catholic friend who will be able to walk with you and guide you in how to grow as an intentional disciple of Jesus.

As we will discuss in the following chapter, the next part of your journey is just beginning—and it can't be done alone.

SMALL GROUP QUESTIONS

1. When you hear the words, "God desires the whole of you," what comes to mind?

2. Why do you think it's necessary to experience true repentance before you can become an intentional follower of Jesus? Put it in your own words, based on your own experience. How would you explain this to a family member or friend who wants to grow closer to Jesus but isn't sure where to begin?

3. Many of us, especially those who were raised Catholic, may have a very negative view of repentance. Maybe we're scared of it because we think it will be painful. Maybe we think repentance is just for really "big" sinners, and we think we're pretty good people. Has this chapter changed this perception for you? If so, how?

4. Maybe it has never occurred to you that you have a "junk room" in your life. If you're still struggling with this concept, is there at least one painful memory, one habit, or one past action that you can surrender to the Lord?

5. What was the experience of handing to Jesus the things of your heart like for you? What are you experiencing now, after doing so?

CHAPTER 8

Jesus Gives Us His Spirit

Jesus makes a promise to his disciples.

Before he goes to his death on the cross, while they are gathered together for the Last Supper, he tells them he is about to leave them. His closest friends, rejoicing in their teacher, master, and friend, now grieve because of his words. Their grief is so great that they cannot grasp the promise he is making to them:

> If you love me, you will keep my commandments. And I will ask the Father, and he will give you another Advocate to be with you always, the Spirit of truth, which the world cannot accept, because it neither sees nor knows it. But you know it, because it remains with you, and will be in you. I will not leave you orphans; I will come to you. (John 14:15–18)

Jesus promises that he will never leave us orphaned, cast out, isolated, or alone. Those who love Jesus will receive his Spirit—the Spirit of God—who will not just stand beside them but will dwell *within* them. In this promise, we hear the echoes of the earliest part of the Great Story in Genesis, when the Father created Adam and "breathed" life into him. Remember that the Hebrew word *ruah* holds a multitude of meanings, including "spirit." The divine life, which Adam and Eve received from God and lost through their disobedience, will be restored in Jesus Christ through the coming of his Spirit.

Even before his death, Jesus reveals the truth of his coming resurrection and the resurrected life that his disciples will receive: "In a little while the world will no longer see me, but you will see me, because I live and you will live" (John 14:19). Recognizing the grief in his disciples, Jesus reassures them further, saying: "But I tell you the truth, it is better for you that I go. For if I do not go, the Advocate will not come to you. But if I go, I will send him to you" (John 16:7). The resurrected life, the life of the kingdom, will come to them in the Spirit. The One who rules the kingdom in love must return to his throne so that his Spirit can establish kingdom life in all of creation and fill the disciples with that very same life. The apostle Paul recognized this when he wrote, "For the kingdom of God is not a matter of food and drink, but of righteousness, peace, and joy in the holy Spirit" (Romans 14:17). The heart of the kingdom is found in the presence, power, and life of the Holy Spirit.

Before the disciples can witness effectively to the love of the Father in Jesus Christ, they must receive the promise of the Father, which is the Holy Spirit. Throughout the Great Story of salvation, the Lord has been preparing his people for the coming of the kingdom in Jesus. For example, though conscious of his people's failure to keep the covenants he made with them, the Lord sent the prophet Ezekiel to let the Israelites know that a time was coming when "I will give you a new heart, and a new spirit I will put within you. I will remove the heart of stone from your flesh and give you a heart of flesh. I will put my spirit within you so that you walk in my statutes, observe my ordinances, and keep them" (Ezekiel 36:26–27).

The Holy Spirit, then, is the promise and reality of the eternal life of the kingdom made manifest in all of creation, particularly in those men and women who receive that Spirit in Jesus Christ. What we experience in the Spirit—right relationship with God, peace, and joy—are all characteristics of kingdom life, a life that brings healing and restoration to our souls. So powerful is this restoration that Paul, acknowledging the work of the Holy Spirit in him, writes, "Whoever is in Christ is a new creation: the old things have passed away; behold, new things have come" (2 Corinthians 5:17). The Spirit of God fills the disciple with the resurrected life of Jesus, which re-creates the one who has received him. This is not just a change of one's actions, or even a transformation of thinking—rather, this is a fundamental transformation of identity.

Again, Paul highlights this reality when he writes:

For those who are led by the Spirit of God are children of God. For you did not receive a spirit of slavery to fall back into fear, but you received a spirit of adoption, through which we cry, "*Abba*, Father!" The Spirit itself bears witness with our spirit that we are children of God, and if children, then heirs, heirs of God and joint heirs with Christ, if only we suffer with him so that we may also be glorified with him. (Romans 8:14)

We who set ourselves in opposition to God—whether intentionally or unintentionally in our daily acts of resistance to his grace and love—can become his children, welcomed fully into his household, through the power of the Spirit in Jesus Christ. The more we live out of that identity as God's children, the more we become truly who the Father created us to be, and the more kingdom life penetrates not only into our own daily experience, but into the lives of those with whom we come in contact. This deepening "penetration of kingdom life" manifests as very concrete fruit in our lives. The truth of God shows us who we really are, and the power of his Spirit allows us to live that reality.

The Holy Spirit is not an idea, a concept, or even a feeling of peace or happiness. The Spirit is a Person, the Third Person of the Trinity. An encounter with the Holy Spirit is an encounter with God, and the presence of the Holy Spirit within us is the presence of the raw, untamed power of the love of God. Power—that's a good word to use here. Scripture uses that word a lot. Often, the New Testament uses the Greek word for power, *dunamis*. It comes from the same root that we use for words like "dynamite" and "dynamic." When we talk about the presence and power of the Holy Spirit, we are talking about the dynamic, life-changing power of God at work within us and within the world. Jesus himself, after his resurrection, instructed his disciples: "And [behold] I am sending the promise of my Father upon you; but stay in the city until you are clothed with **power** from on high" (Luke 24:49, emphasis added).

In the power of the Holy Spirit, we receive new hearts. The Lord changes our identity and gives us the capability to live that identity out, to become like him. The Spirit, then, produces fruit in us. Paul talks about this kind of fruit in his letter to the Church at Galatia: "The fruit of the Spirit is love, joy, peace, patience, kindness, generosity, faithfulness, gentleness, self-control" (Galatians 5:22–23). Those to whom the kingdom is given receive freedom and power to live that kingdom life. We become more and more configured to Christ, and we experience deeper and deeper freedom to respond in love to the circumstances and people in our lives. In short, we grow in holiness through the presence of the Spirit within us.

The Lord also promised his Spirit through the prophet Joel, who revealed to the people of Judah the ultimate vindication of the promises of their God when he wrote: "It shall come to pass / I will pour out my spirit upon all flesh. / Your sons and daughters will prophesy, / your old men will dream dreams, / your young men will see visions. / Even upon your male and female servants, / in those days, I will pour out my spirit" (Joel 3:1–2). In those days, the Spirit rested on just a few: the prophets, the judges of Israel, and the righteous men and women. Here, Joel is prophesying about an outpouring of God's Spirit on all of humanity. When this happens, the Spirit will not only produce fruit *in* us, but also *through* us, for the sake of others.

Again, Paul highlights this power of God working through those who have received him:

There are different kinds of spiritual gifts but the same Spirit; there are different forms of service but the same Lord; there are different workings but the same God who produces all of them in everyone. To each individual the manifestation of the Spirit is

given for some benefit. To one is given through the
Spirit the expression of wisdom; to another the expression of knowledge according to the same Spirit;
to another faith by the same Spirit; to another gifts of
healing by the one Spirit; to another mighty deeds; to
another prophecy; to another discernment of spirits;
to another varieties of tongues; to another interpretation of tongues. But one and the same Spirit produces all of these, distributing them individually to
each person as he wishes. (1 Corinthians 12:4–11)

These gifts enable ordinary men and women to become
extraordinary channels of God's presence, love, healing, and
power for the sake of others. They empower the work of
the Church and help others to encounter the kingdom of
God in Jesus Christ. This is why Jesus, referring to John the
Baptist, the last prophet of the Old Covenant, said, "I tell you,
among those born of women, no one is greater than John;
yet the least in the kingdom of God is greater than he" (Luke
7:28). The heirs of the kingdom, those who have received
the promise of God's Spirit in Jesus Christ, bear the divine
life, not simply alongside of them, but within them, as part of
their renewed and re-created nature.

THE FULFILLMENT OF THE PROMISE

Fifty days after Jesus' death and resurrection during the Jew-
ish feast of Passover, the disciples are gathered in the Upper
Room for the Jewish feast of Pentecost. The last instruction
Jesus gave them before his ascension is still ringing in their

ears: "Stay in the city until you are clothed with power from on high" (Luke 24:49). The disciples have locked themselves in the Upper Room "for fear of the Jews" (John 20:19). Since Jesus' arrest, they have been ruled by fear and grief, and even though they have seen the risen Jesus, they are still baffled, disoriented, and afraid. Most of us can relate to their feelings of abandonment and anxiety, their sense of being alone in their weakness, unsure of what's coming next.

In an instant, all of that changes for the disciples: "Suddenly there came from the sky a noise like a strong driving wind, and it filled the entire house in which they were. Then there appeared to them tongues as of fire, which parted and came to rest on each one of them. And they were all filled with the holy Spirit and began to speak in different tongues, as the Spirit enabled them to proclaim" (Acts 2:2–4). From that moment the disciples are filled with the resurrected life of Jesus Christ, through the power of the Holy Spirit. They spill out of the Upper Room and boldly proclaim the good news of God's saving love in Jesus Christ. They are guided by this Spirit, empowered to preach, to heal, and to raise the dead. They become more like Christ, willing to give their lives in service to others, because of the work of the Spirit within them.

This is the birthright of every Christian. To be a coheir with Christ (see Romans 8:14) is to receive the gift of kingdom life from the Father. This gift, an experience of mercy, love, healing, forgiveness, and renewal that restores our identity and transforms the whole of our lives, immerses us in the resurrected power of Christ through the Spirit. Now our lives can become a sign and channel of God's redeeming love, just as the disciples' lives were. The Holy Spirit speaks to our hearts, providing guidance, consolation, protection, healing, and empowerment for this life.

How then, do we receive this great gift from Jesus?

RECEIVING THE HOLY SPIRIT

Nicodemus, a Pharisee and secret disciple of Jesus, came to talk with the Lord at night. He desired to know more about the kingdom of God. Jesus told him, "No one can see the kingdom of God without being born from above" (John 3:3). This confused Nicodemus, who still saw things from an earthly perspective. He wondered how someone who was already born could somehow be born again. Jesus clarified his original statement: "Amen, amen, I say to you, no one can enter the kingdom of God without being born of water and Spirit" (John 3:5).

Jesus here refers to Baptism. The word itself comes from the Greek word *baptizein*, which can mean to plunge, immerse, and overwhelm. In the waters of Baptism, we are plunged, or immersed, into the death of Christ, so that we may rise from the waters immersed in his life, which we receive in the Spirit. Thus Paul writes, "We were indeed buried with him through baptism into death, so that, just as Christ was raised from the dead by the glory of the Father, we too might live in newness of life" (Romans 6:4). Therefore, the normative way one is "born from above" and born into the kingdom is through the Sacrament of Baptism. Those who are baptized have been plunged or immersed, not only into the mercy of God, not only into his kindness and love, but also into his very life, the life of the Trinity—kingdom life.

If you have not yet been baptized, continue through to the next chapters of the Great Story. What you need to begin that journey is given there.

If you have already been baptized, then you have already received the gift of kingdom life, and the promise of the Holy Spirit has been given to you. Maybe that is surprising to you. So many of our baptized brothers and sisters have received kingdom life in Jesus Christ through the power of the Holy Spirit, but they don't even know it. They have been re-created and made new, but the testimony and experience of their own lives does not bear that out. They feel trapped, powerless against the temptations that seem to barrage them. God feels distant, and the weight of their own brokenness and imperfections hangs around them like a thick chain. Or worse, they soldier on through life unaware that there could be any relief or recourse to change.

How can that be?

The reality is that the sacraments (like Baptism) are not magic. Although the sacraments are particular encounters with Christ, as well as efficacious in bringing about what they signify, they require something from us. That is not to say, objectively, our human action empowers the sacraments in any way. The sacraments are purely the action and work of God upon us. However, because we have received the gift of free will, we can choose to reject the grace of God at work in the sacraments, either explicitly or implicitly, through the countless decisions we make each day.

Many of us were baptized as infants. At the moment of our Baptism, our parents' faith stood in for us. We received the gift of new life in the Holy Spirit. Once we grew older, the Lord, who desires authentic and real relationship with each person, awaited our personal response. Many Catholics have never been taught that, or they have never understood it. Some Catholics know about a personal response but do not know how to go about giving it.

Wherever you are coming from, the truth is that God intends for you to experience the power of his kingdom life now. That life, which is a life lived in the Spirit of God, is your birthright. The Holy Spirit isn't secondary or optional for Catholics. The Lord desires that all of us grow in his Spirit. The Holy Spirit also desires to be in a relationship with each of us. This means that life in the Spirit, life in the kingdom, is about an ever-greater yielding to the presence of the Holy Spirit within us, and a deeper intimacy with him that will produce an even deeper fidelity to the Father in the person of Jesus Christ.

If you want to experience the power of God's kingdom in your life, if you are ready to begin or deepen your friendship with God and cooperate with his Spirit, then turn the page. The Great Story involves you—in a deeply intimate way.

FURTHER REFLECTION

Although the Spirit is a Person and an equal member of the Trinity, many of us don't foster an intimate, personal relationship with him. Fortunately, he is always ready to respond when we ask. I encourage you to begin to invite him in during your prayer time this week. Here are a few steps to get you started:

- As you begin to pray, specifically invite the Holy Spirit into your prayer time. You can pray the Come, Holy

Spirit Prayer: "Come Holy Spirit, fill the hearts of your faithful and kindle in them the fire of your love. Send forth your Spirit and they shall be created. And you shall renew the face of the earth. O, God, who by the light of the Holy Spirit, did instruct the hearts of the faithful, grant that by the same Holy Spirit we may be truly wise and ever enjoy his consolations, through Christ Our Lord, Amen." You can make this prayer a very personal one by saying things like, "Fill my heart and kindle in it the fire of your love." Or you can pray spontaneously and just invite the Holy Spirit to be with you as you pray.

- During your prayer time, ask the Holy Spirit to open your heart more to Christ, to give you the grace to become more of an intentional disciple of the Son.

- Thank the Holy Spirit for his presence during your prayer time and ask him to help you hear his voice more clearly in your life.

We can also use specific prayers to invite the Holy Spirit to draw us deeper into a relationship with him. The following prayer is an ancient one, attributed to St. Augustine of Hippo. Some of its language may seem a bit formal, so feel free to change in a way that will make you feel more comfortable:

Prayer for the Indwelling of the Spirit
Holy Spirit, powerful Consoler, sacred Bond of the Father and the Son, Hope of the afflicted, descend into my heart and establish in it your loving dominion. Enkindle in my tepid soul the fire of your Love so that I may be wholly subject to you. We believe

that when you dwell in us, you also prepare a dwelling for the Father and the Son. Deign, therefore, to come to me, Consoler of abandoned souls, and Protector of the needy. Help the afflicted, strengthen the weak, and support the wavering. Come and purify me. Let no evil desire take possession of me. You love the humble and resist the proud. Come to me, glory of the living, and hope of the dying. Lead me by your grace that I may always be pleasing to you. Amen.

SMALL GROUP QUESTIONS

1. What has your relationship with the Holy Spirit consisted of up until this point? How do you hope to see that changed now?

2. Have you ever prayed to the Holy Spirit? If so, what was the situation and what happened? If not, why not?

3. What are some concrete ways you can invite the Holy Spirit to take a more active part in your daily life? Where do you think he is asking you to let him in?

4. When you think of the power that comes with God's kingdom life, what comes to your mind? Do you want this power to be unleashed in and through your own life? If yes, why? If not, why?

5. Do you think it is really possible to become like Christ through the power of the Holy Spirit? What do you think keeps people (you) from experiencing that trans-formation?

6. What are some fears or reservations that people may have at the idea of experiencing a release of the Spirit in their lives?

CHAPTER 9

Jesus Calls Us into a Life of Discipleship

Saying "yes" to Jesus looks like something.

The Great Story doesn't end with our repentance—it begins there. Although the working of God in each human heart is a mystery, Jesus calls us to something tangible. Our initial conscious choice to accept Jesus as Lord is the first step in a larger journey—an adventure that will change the scope and direction of our entire lives.

When Jesus called the Twelve Apostles, he invited each of them to follow him, and that call is extended to every human person. The words that Jesus uses to call us are active, not passive: "Then Jesus said to his disciples, 'Whoever wishes to come after me must deny himself, take up his cross, and follow me'" (Matthew 16:24). If we want to live as disciples we must "deny," "take up," and "follow." There is an intentionality to discipleship. One doesn't become a disciple simply by birth, cultural affiliation, or profession. We aren't necessarily disciples because we were born into a Catholic family, or because we are Irish (or any other ethnicity), or even because we work for the Church. Discipleship emerges out of a sus-

tained encounter with the Lord in the midst of his Church
and a conscious decision to choose Christ each day.

Sherry Weddell, in her landmark book, *Forming Intentional Disciples*, writes on how we become disciples:

> By acting like Simon Peter: "Jesus said to Simon, 'Do
> not be afraid; henceforth you will be catching men.'
> And when they had brought their boats to land, they
> left everything and followed him." (Luke 5:10–11)

> Simon's experience was not exceptional, either in
> human terms or in the tradition of the Church.
> No one voluntarily sheds his or her job, home, and
> whole way of life accidentally or unconsciously. Si-
> mon Peter's "drop the net decision" is what we mean
> by disciple. From the moment he dropped his nets to
> follow Jesus, he was a disciple.[14]

The Great Story of Jesus, although it has cosmic dimen-
sions, penetrates into the personal, into the heart of every
man, woman, and child with ears to hear. When we respond
with an openness of heart, when we say "yes" to what the
Great Story, and the One who is at the center of that story,
offers us, the path of discipleship opens up to us.

The word "disciple" comes from Latin, and it means "one
who learns." In the culture of Jesus' time, a disciple sat at
the foot of a rabbi (teacher) and learned from him. Disciples
were also expected to take on the lifestyle of the one they

---

[14] Sherry Weddell, *Forming Intentional Disciples* (Huntington, IN: Our
Sunday Visitor, 2012), 65.

followed, absorbing not only knowledge but their rabbi's way of life. Both in his interaction with the original twelve disciples and now with each of us, Jesus keeps this dimension of discipleship and goes a step further. Jesus doesn't simply want his disciples to *act* like him, rather we are invited to *become* like him. We do this through the outpouring of his life, which comes to us through the power of the Holy Spirit.

Christian disciples, then, are men and women who have heard the Great Story of Jesus, who have allowed it to penetrate and enter the circumstances of their lives, and who have given themselves over to Jesus. In this way, they bear that story (and the one who sits at its center) within them and become heralds of that story to everyone they meet. St. Paul talks about this in a related way when he writes, "We are ambassadors for Christ, as if God were appealing through us" (2 Corinthians 5:20). The power of the Great Story is the reality of the kingdom lived out in the daily rhythms of life.

DISCIPLESHIP AND THE
DISCIPLINES OF FOLLOWING JESUS

Our journey through the Great Story is almost at an end, but your own journey in Christ, the specific ways that this story intersects with your own personal story, continues. How will you, in your own journey of discipleship, experience the power of God's kingdom and make that kingdom present in the lives of others?

The Church exists so that the kingdom life offered by Jesus might be made more manifest in the world. Recall that we live in the time between the inauguration of the kingdom of

God here on earth and its fulfillment at the end of time, when God's kingdom will manifest in its full power and perfection. Thus the Church is more than a collection of institutional units (parishes and dioceses) that organize and deploy its resources. Rather, the Church is the reality of the kingdom planted in the world, like a seed. The Church and all her members, by their presence within the world, should radiate, manifest, and intentionally share the kingdom life they have received from Christ in and through the power of the Holy Spirit. As we allow kingdom life to penetrate more deeply in us, we experience not only greater freedom and conformity to Jesus, but we become even more effective channels of that kingdom for others. God's life spills out of us into the lives of those whom we encounter. Discipleship is the living out of this reality both in community and in the context of our own life.

The gift of God's Spirit is given so that we might bear fruit in this journey of discipleship (see John 15:8). In the introduction to his book *Follow Christ*, Dave Nodar talks about this kind of growth:

> It is critically important in reading the New Testament to see that following Christ is based on God's initiative—his love for us, the forgiveness of sins, and the gift of the Holy Spirit. He sanctifies and empowers us to move outward and share the good news. The Christian life is based on the grace of God that empowers us ***AND* on our response and effort to mature in doing his will**.[15] (emphasis in original)

---

[15] Dave Nodar, Father Erik Arnold, and Ally Ascosi, *Follow Christ* (Huntington, IN: Our Sunday Visitor, 2016), 7-8.

We respond to, and cooperate with, the Holy Spirit when we live out, with his help, the disciplines of a follower of Jesus. The more faithfully we live these disciplines out, the more God's grace transforms us and the more fruitful we become as his disciples. The word "discipline" sometimes gets a bad "rap" in our society. For many it evokes the image of punishment or consequences. For others, it recalls a kind of obligation or burden placed upon them. If we think of people we know who are successful in a particular field, however—whether in business, education, health care, or any number of endeavors—they most likely exhibit a kind of discipline, a focused attention on and regular practice of, the core elements essential to mastering their particular profession.

Perhaps the clearest example comes from the world of athletics. Look at the dedication, discipline, and focus required of elite gymnasts. In order to master the complex skills required for them to achieve success, these athletes must shape their whole day around practice—this includes getting up early and putting hour after hour in at the gym, but it also includes their diet and even how they rest. Their whole life revolves around the disciplines associated with their chosen sport. Paul uses this idea of an athlete as a metaphor for the life of discipleship when he writes:

Do you not know that the runners in the stadium all run in the race, but only one wins the prize? Run so as to win. Every athlete exercises discipline in every way. They do it to win a perishable crown, but we an imperishable one. Thus I do not run aimlessly; I do not fight as if I were shadowboxing. No, I drive my body and train it, for fear that, after having preached to others, I myself should be disqualified. (1 Corinthians 9:24–27)

The incredible news about the disciplines of following Christ is that we do not need to rely solely on our own willpower, strength, or human abilities to grow as disciples. Growth in Christ comes through our cooperation with the Holy Spirit. We have received the very life of God, which the Church calls grace, in the Sacrament of Baptism. That grace is sealed and strengthened in Confirmation, restored in Reconciliation, and grows within us every time we receive the Lord with openness of heart in holy Communion. Even the very desire to grow as a follower in Christ comes to us through the power and presence of the Holy Spirit at work in our lives. All we need to do is say "yes" to that desire through concrete acts of discipleship. The best part is, growing in each of the disciplines of following Christ makes it easier to say "yes" to those disciplines the next time. The road won't always be easy, and the Lord will call us to surrender ourselves more and more to him, but we have received every grace we need to persevere fruitfully.

So, what are the disciplines of discipleship? While a full exploration of each of these disciplines is worthy of a book in itself, there are a few simple things we can outline here to get started.

Daily Scripture Reading: The Bible is the very Word of God and, along with the teaching of the apostles, makes up the foundation of the Christian faith. The author of the Book of Hebrews had this to say about the power of the Word of God: "Indeed, the word of God is living and effective, sharper than any two-edged sword, penetrating even between soul and spirit, joints and marrow, and able to discern reflections and thoughts of the heart" (4:12). Through the power of the Holy Spirit, we encounter the risen and living Jesus in a personal way when we read the Scriptures. God's desire is to meet us, speak to us, instruct us, console us, and challenge and transform us in and through our reading of Scripture EVERY SINGLE DAY.

If you grew up Catholic, you may have the sense that someone told you not to read the Bible, or discouraged you from picking it up. Or you may have had a very large, coffee-table Bible in your home that seemed too ornamental or unwieldy to sit and read. Or perhaps the Bible just seems too difficult to understand, and that makes you uncomfortable to try it. The reality is that the Bible is accessible, and reading it is an essential part of being a disciple. If you are not sure how to start reading the Bible, then I suggest beginning with the Gospel of Mark in the New Testament. It is the shortest of the four Gospels, and you can take fifteen minutes each day and read just one chapter a day, asking the Lord to open your heart to his voice before you read it. You can also use the suggested Scripture passages at the end of each chapter of this book.

It is important to read Scripture with "the mind of the Church," meaning that we are to read the Bible connected to the Church's teaching authority. It is equally important to read Scripture with the "ears of the heart" in order to begin to discern the voice of God as he speaks to us through his Word. This is more than simply learning the Scriptures through participating in a Bible study (though taking advantage of Bible-study groups can be very important as you grow in Christ). It means reading with a prayerful attitude of receptivity, listening with the ears of your heart for whatever God wants to say to you specifically.

Daily Prayer: At the heart of the kingdom is relationship—intimacy, encounter, and communion. Jesus lived that out on earth through his daily times of prayer. Prayer unites our heart with God's heart, allowing us to spend time with the One whom we are growing to love more deeply. Before I married my wife, we spent time together, getting to know each other and growing in intimacy. Prayer is simply getting to know God. It can come in many forms. There are standard rote prayers that we say (the Our Father, or the Hail Mary, for example). There are devotions (like the Rosary, or the Stations of the Cross). There are more formal liturgical prayers (like the Mass, or the Divine Office). Prayer can occur anywhere and at any time throughout the day. What it requires is some focused time with the Lord.

In prayer, we engage in a dialogue with the Lord. While it is definitely important that we speak to the Lord what is on our hearts, it is also critical that we learn how to hear his response. There are many books and resources on prayer, but there is no substitute for being personally formed by someone who understands this discipline. Your pastor, another priest, a deacon, or any other member of your parish's staff can be a great resource in teaching you how to pray.

One of the best ways to build up a daily habit of prayer is to create a small space in your home where you can spend time praying. Placing a crucifix, sacred art, or other images that help you recall God's love can make it easier to enter into prayer. Another helpful tip is to try and make your prayer time consistent every day. I used to run pretty regularly, about every two days. I was always amazed at how, on the mornings of my scheduled day to run, my body would prepare itself for the exertion of running. I would wake up and my heart rate would slow, my breathing deepen. The same holds true in the spiritual life. The more consistent we are in our prayer times, the more prepared we are in our spirit to come to God in prayer.

Once you have settled on a time and a place to pray, just start by spending ten minutes or so in prayer each day. Perhaps you can begin with a song that leads you to think about God, and then begin to talk with God. Thank him for the day and let him know what you are thinking, feeling, and experiencing right at that moment. Then ask the Holy Spirit to quiet your heart and just listen for the Lord's response to you in prayer. After the first week, add another five minutes to your prayer time. Of course, you can use this time to pray with more formal prayers and devotions—like the Rosary. Just be sure to take the time to listen to the Lord as you pray.

Living a Sacramental Life: As we mentioned earlier, the sacraments are particular and effective encounters with Jesus Christ. When we participate in and celebrate the sacraments, we receive an outpouring of God's life that changes us, helping us to become holy and more like Christ. A disciple lives a conscious sacramental life, which means regular weekly (and sometimes daily) attendance at Mass, as well as frequent reception of the Sacrament of Reconciliation. Simply put, a disciple does not stay away from the sacraments.

If it has been a while since you went to Mass or Confession, I want to encourage you to return. Discipleship is an experience of kingdom life, of communion and relationship with God. Our sin and brokenness can interfere with that relationship. In his goodness, God pours out more of his life for us in the sacraments so we can be restored again. When you fall in your journey with Christ, there is no condemnation. Instead, the Father invites us to receive his mercy again and again in the sacraments. With his grace, we are restored. He lifts us up and sets us on the path again—and we receive his power to deal with the temptations and obstacles we encounter.

Fellowship: Membership in the Church is not like membership in a club, or a nonprofit, volunteer, or civic organization. The baptized are incorporated into Christ's body and share a bond that goes far deeper than even the natural bond that joins the human race together. The experience of life in the kingdom is not solitary but communal, characterized by mutuality and interdependence. As we have mentioned previously, communion with God by definition includes communion with all who are in relationship to him. Thus the call to relationship with Christ as a disciple is a call into community or deep fellowship. Because of Christ, our lives no longer make any sense apart from one another. Therefore, as baptized brothers and sisters in the Lord, we must live out this deep fellowship in community, provide support for one another, and even go out and serve the world together. I like to say that Christians are like charcoal briquettes—we burn hotter, brighter, and longer when we remain connected.

This kind of fellowship goes beyond just coffee and donuts after Mass, or participation in the occasional pancake breakfast. This kind of fellowship is a sharing of our life in

Christ together. One of the most powerful expressions of this kind of fellowship can be found in what are called small faith communities or Christian small groups. These are small gatherings of Christians, usually in a home or at the parish, who get together to pray, learn, laugh, and support one another. I strongly encourage you to find one of these groups and join.

Service: Disciples must live out the radical self-offering of Jesus by offering our very selves for the sake of the world—especially for the poor and suffering. Not simply out of altruism, volunteerism, or on ethical and moral grounds, but foundationally because we know that Christ is present in each human person and God holds a special place in his heart for those who are poor and suffering. The call to service is found in one of the most recognizable passages in the New Testament, John 3:16: "For God so loved the world that he gave his only Son, so that everyone who believes in him might not perish but have eternal life." God's love for the world was so great that he GAVE. If we, then, profess to follow him and hold his life within us, then how can we not give for the sake of others? This kind of giving includes acts of charity and mercy, but it also encompasses applying Gospel values to issues of injustice in the world today. Where are those issues in your local community or neighborhood? Where is Christ present to you in the poor and the unwanted? How can you bring the power of the kingdom to bear for the person in need whom you encounter?

Evangelization (Sharing Christ): The heart of the Church's mission is to share Christ with others, to make Christ present in word and deed so the kingdom of God manifests powerfully in the world. When we encounter Christ, we encounter the One for whom our hearts were made, and we discover who we are, our purpose, and our destiny. This is an experience the Lord wants all of his children to have, not a special few.

At some point, as kingdom life takes hold of you, your life will begin to change—and people will notice. When they ask questions, when they want to know what has happened to you, tell them! You don't need a theology degree or advanced training. If you are excited about what you believe and what that belief has done for your life, then talk about it. At its most basic, evangelization is helping others encounter the Jesus to whom we have given ourselves.

A WORD OF ENCOURAGEMENT

If some (or all) of these disciplines seem overwhelming at the moment, have no fear. If, after wrestling with and reflecting on the Great Story of Jesus, your relationship with God has changed and deepened, know that the Lord doesn't expect perfection from you tomorrow. Nor is there condemnation if you start walking this path of discipleship and stumble. A good and perfect Father, he is patient with his children and offers forgiveness and strength as we remain in him.

Also, know that none of these disciplines can be "mastered" in isolation. Just like it would be impossible to learn advanced gymnastics moves from watching a YouTube video or reading a manual, you cannot expect to grow deeply in these disciplines from just reading about them. Books and video resources on each of these elements of discipleship abound, but they require the input, experience, coaching, and accompaniment of others. Look for disciple-friends and mentors who can walk with you on this path, and when the time comes, be open and willing to walk with others.

Finally, I want to leave you with these words from St. Paul:

> Rejoice in the Lord always. I shall say it again: rejoice! Your kindness should be known to all. The Lord is near. Have no anxiety at all, but in everything, by prayer and petition, with thanksgiving, make your requests known to God. Then the peace of God that surpasses all understanding will guard your hearts and minds in Christ Jesus.
>
> Finally, brothers, whatever is true, whatever is honorable, whatever is just, whatever is pure, whatever is lovely, whatever is gracious, if there is any excellence and if there is anything worthy of praise, think about these things. Keep on doing what you have learned and received and heard and seen in me. Then the God of peace will be with you. (Philippians 4:4–9)

The Great Story of Jesus hasn't ended. It continues on now in you. You are the manifestation of the Lord's love for all whom you meet. In your own way, in the simple rhythms of your life, the Father is reaching out to his children and calling them back to himself in Christ Jesus.

How amazing a gift the Lord has given you.

How grace-filled your response.

How beautiful you are—in him.

APPENDIX

Summary of the Great Story

As we journey forward as followers of Christ, we may find it helpful to reflect again on the beauty and shape of the Great Story. Certainly, as we follow the command of Christ to "make disciples of all nations" (Matthew 28:19) we will need to know this story well enough to share it. Below is a quick summary of the Great Story of Jesus.

The Great Story began in communion. Adam and Eve lived in perfect relationship with God, each other, and the whole of creation, stemming from the divine life which they received from God. This is what God originally intended for all of us—an experience of intimacy and union with him that would never end. This is the kingdom of God.

Adam and Eve's disobedience ruptured that perfect relationship. Because they were the first human beings, their fall deprived all of us of divine life, separating us from the One who created us. Sin, death, illness, and suffering entered into human life. In his goodness, God himself came to set the situation right. The Father sent the Son to call the whole human race back to himself. Through his life, death, resurrection, and ascension Jesus satisfied the Father's justice and mercy, paying the price for sin and making the divine life—the life of the kingdom—once more present in creation and available to all who desire it. Now Jesus invites each of us to receive a share in his very own life, lived in communion with the Father through the power of the Holy Spirit. Thanks to Jesus' redeeming work, we are all sons and daughters of the Father.

Jesus makes this kingdom life freely available to us as a gift. All we need to do is turn away from sin (repent), offer God our hearts, and receive Baptism. In this way we are made new, and we become part of Christ's body, the Church. Co-operating with the love, mercy, and grace we receive through the sacraments, we grow more like Christ as his disciples and represent him to the world, manifesting the love and power of the kingdom in the ordinary circumstances of life. Thus the Church is the seed of the kingdom, already present in creation and bearing fruit, yet awaiting the time when Christ will come again and the kingdom of God will be present in its fullness.